"YOU THINK IT STRANGE,

—LEGENDARY ENGLISH SEER MOTHER SHIPTON (1488–1561)

JEANNE DIXON . . .
Envisioned 1962 as the birth year of the Antichrist.

NOSTRADAMUS . . .
Predicted his zenith: 1999 and seven months.

EDGAR CAYCE . . .
Foresaw the Second World War—and the natural destruction of
Los Angeles and New York by the year 2000.

PROPHECY OF WARSAW . . .
Accurately anticipated the Napoleonic Wars, and the forthcoming
disaster of an earthbound comet.

OUR LADY OF FATIMA . . .
Made three prophecies in 1917. Two have been fulfilled. The third,
and most dire, has been concealed from the public in the Secret
Vatican Archives.

PROPHECIES:
2000

By the same author

Encyclopedia of the Roman Empire

The Vampire Encyclopedia

Encyclopedia Sherlockiana

The Angelic Doctor:
The Life and World of St. Thomas Aquinas

Our Sunday Visitor's Encyclopedia
of Catholic History

The Pope Encyclopedia

Encyclopedia of the Middle Ages

Papal Wisdom:
Words of Hope and Inspiration
from Pope John Paul II

The Wisdom Teachings of
the Dalai Lama

PROPHECIES:
2000

PREDICTIONS, REVELATIONS, AND VISIONS FOR THE NEW MILLENNIUM

MATTHEW BUNSON

POCKET BOOKS
New York   London   Toronto   Sydney   Tokyo   Singapore

An Original Publication of POCKET BOOKS

POCKET BOOKS, a division of Simon & Schuster Inc.
1230 Avenue of the Americas, New York, NY 10020

Bunson, Matthew.
     Prophecies 2000: predictions, revelations, and
     visions for the new millennium / Matthew Bunson.
          p.   cm.
     Includes bibliographical references.
     ISBN   0-671-01917-1
          1. Twenty-first century—Forecasts—Quotations, maxims, etc.
     I. Title.   II. Title: Prophecies two thousand.
CB161.B86   1999
303.49—dc21   98-51027
                                                    CIP

First Pocket Books trade paperback printing January 1999

10 9 8 7 6 5 4 3 2

Cover design by Mike Stromberg

Printed in the U.S.A.

This book is dedicated to the many who will not see the new millennium. This work is also dedicated to the memory of Erika Cheetham, scholar and one of our age's foremost experts on the life and writings of Nostradamus.

ACKNOWLEDGMENTS

There are many people to whom a debt of gratitude is owed for their kind assistance in the preparation of this work. Among them are: the staffs of several libraries, including the Sahara West Library; Kim Clanton-Green; Marie Cuglietta; Elke Villa; Stephen Bunson; Margaret Bunson; my exceedingly patient agent, Martha Casselman; and most of all Jane Cavolina, my editor. Thank you, Jane, for making this book a reality, for rescuing it from the brink of oblivion, and most of all for your friendship and vast skills as an editor.

The Seven Angels of the Apocalypse

The seven angels that had the seven trumpets now made ready to sound them. The first blew his trumpet and, with that, hail and fire, mixed with blood, were dropped on the earth: a third of the earth was burned up, and a third of all trees, and every blade of grass was burned.

The second angel blew his trumpet, and it was as though a great mountain all on fire had been dropped into the sea: a third of the sea turned to blood, a third of all living things in the sea were killed, and a third of all ships were destroyed.

The third angel blew his trumpet, and a huge star fell from the sky, burning like a ball of fire, and it fell on a third of all rivers and springs; this was the star called Wormwood, and a third of all water turned to bitter wormwood, so that many people died from drinking it.

The fourth angel blew his trumpet, and a third of the sun and a third of the moon and a third of the stars were blasted, so that the light went out of a third of them and for a third of the day there was no illumination, and the same with the night . . .

Then the fifth angel blew his trumpet, and I saw a star that had fallen from heaven onto the earth, and he was given the key to the shaft leading down to the Abyss. When he unlocked the shaft of the Abyss, smoke poured up out of the Abyss like the smoke from a huge furnace so that the sun and the sky were darkened by it . . .

The sixth angel blew his trumpet, and I heard a voice come out of the four horns of the golden altar in front of God. It spoke to the sixth angel with the trumpet, and said "Release the four angels that are chained up at the great river Euphrates." These four angels had been put there ready for this hour of this day of this month of this year, and now they were released to destroy a third of the human race.

Then I saw another powerful angel coming down from heaven, wrapped in cloud, with a rainbow over his head; his face was like the sun, and his legs were pillars of fire. In his hand he had a small scroll, unrolled; he put his right foot in the sea and his left foot on the land and he shouted so loud, it was like a lion roaring . . . "The time of waiting is over; at the time when the seventh angel is heard sounding his trumpet, God's secret intention will be fulfilled . . ."

FROM THE BOOK OF REVELATION

CONTENTS

Introduction: *First Vespers for the Millennium*   xiii

Part One: Prophecies of Darkness   1

Natural Disasters   3

Wars and Armageddon   28

Plagues and Epidemics   59

The Antichrist   67

Economic Ruin   77

The Papacy   82

Religion   95

Space and Extraterrestrials   116

Part Two: Prophecies of Hope   129

Appendices

The Prophets   143

Biblical Prophecies   161

Apocryphal Writings   164

Marian Apparitions   165

Prophecies of the Popes   167

The End of the World   168

Suggested Reading   171

Introduction:

First Vespers for the Millennium

What seest thou else
In the dark backward and abysm of time?
The Tempest (I.2.49)

The coming of the next millennium is being greeted with a curious mixture of joyous fanfare, nostalgic reflection, and, in many places, fear and trepidation. Even as celebrations will ring the globe—from the loud and brash parties in Times Square, Las Vegas, Rio, and Paris to the solemn and moving Great Jubilee of the Holy Year planned by Pope John Paul II to proclaim the arrival of the third Christian Millennium—many will take a moment to ponder the titanic events of the last hundred years: the wars; political, social, religious, and economic upheaval; and the technological breakthroughs beyond the imaginings of those of previous ages. Equally, just as the year 1000 was anticipated with fear and expectations of the Final Judgment, so too is 2000 seen as a time of atonement, possible terror, and even the end of humanity's dominance on the planet.

The variety of responses and expectations reveals that, at its essence, the dawn of the year 2000 has an individual meaning unique to each person in the world. For many, however, there is a particular sense of expectancy beyond mere musings on the future. There is a longing to know what will come to pass, and the methods that are used are as diverse as the different expectations themselves. There is logic to this, for as Charles Kettering observed in *Seed for Thought:* "We should all be concerned about the future because we will have to spend the rest of our lives there."

It is little wonder, then, that the last years have witnessed an increased interest in prophecies on the millennium, as seen in the sales of books on Nostradamus, Edgar Cayce, and many others. The study of seers and prophets raises the obvious question of how reliable they are in their predictions and whether any of them should be believed. The simplified answer to both questions is that the art of mastering prophecy lies in the interpretation. Some prophecies are seemingly more accurate than others, just as some prophets have reputations for accuracy that exceed others. The prophecies of the Virgin Mary at Fatima in 1917 are ranked among the most significant and urgent for our time. Conversely, other less known prophecies by Mary (such as Bayside and even Medjugorje)—and unrecognized by the official authorities of the Catholic Church—are considered far less accurate.

Interpreting the prophecies of the centuries on the basis of accuracy, normally by the events actually fulfilled, is rendered itself difficult because of disagreement over what exactly a particular prophecy means and whether it even meets the criterion of fulfillment. It is additionally arduous to give meaningful interpretation to a prophecy when, as often happens, it is written in deliberately obscure language and decorated with arcane imagery. The Book of Revelation, cited more than any other prophetic biblical text, is a classic example of baffling symbolism. Nostradamus, meanwhile, used deliberately difficult and enigmatic language to safeguard himself against possible arrest and persecution by authorities, both civil and ecclesiastical.

Prophecies: 2000 is intended to celebrate these two current developments in modern culture. First, it is a recognition of the allure and excitement surrounding the approaching millennium, offering a sampling of prophecies encompassing virtually every area of modern concern, both terrifying and joyous. Second, this book seeks to satisfy, in its own way, the yearning on the part of many to know what to expect in the coming days and years. Unlike many other collections of prophecies, however, no attempt is being made to interpret the prophecies in this volume. Rather, the host of prophecies from across the ages are presented without comment and with translations as faithful to the original languages as possible. Much as the millennium means something particular to each person, so too are the prophecies of the centuries left here to be interpreted according to each reader's individual lights and intuition; it is the reader, an inhabitant of now, who must live in the days of tomorrow, in keeping with Boris Pasternak's observation in *Night:* "You are eternity's hostage. A captive of Time."

Prophecies: 2000 is organized into two main sections: prophecies of a dire and often grim nature about the coming days, and those of a brighter, more promising future.

The prophets presented here come from across the ages and include saints, philosophers, farmers, psychics, popes, novelists, and writings whose authorship are lost to history but whose promises for our time are still all too clear. It will be obvious to readers that the former section is disproportionately larger than the latter. Prophecies are further divided for ease of use into specific topics, such as "Natural Disasters," "Wars and Armageddon," "Religion," and "Plagues and Epidemics." For those who wish to know more about individual prophets, an appendix contains biographical and historical information on virtually all of the prophets quoted or mentioned in the text.

Included in the appendices are sections on biblical prophecies, Marian apparitions, prophecies of popes, and a list of proposed dates for the end of the world. A suggested reading list is included for those interested in works providing interpretation of prophecies from many different perspectives.

PART ONE

Prophecies of Darkness

Natural Disasters

And it shall come to pass that whosoever gets safe out of the war shall die in the earthquake and whosoever gets safe out of the earthquake shall be burned by the fire, and whosoever gets safe out of the fire shall be destroyed by famine.

BOOK OF BARUCH

Earthquakes, hurricanes, floods, tornadoes, droughts, hail, famine. The history of the planet is a long record of natural calamities and terrestrial upheaval—and it is the chronic misfortune of humans to be residents upon such a volatile sphere. Given the natural disasters that have befallen humans over the ages—from the legendary fall of Atlantis to the eruption of Mt. Vesuvius in A.D. 79 that buried Pompeii and Herculaneum beneath a mountain of ash to the earthquakes in China in 1556 that killed nearly a million people—it is little wonder that prophets have beheld visions of impending destruction.

It is estimated that every year about half a million earthquakes rattle the earth. The majority of these are barely felt, but when a major quake hits, entire cities and hundreds of thousands of lives may hang in the balance. Should earthquakes strike along an area such as the Pacific Rim—perhaps in conjunction with the eruptions of the hundreds of volcanoes found in the vast region of the Pacific basin—the resulting damage and loss of life could take decades to repair, cost trillions, and bring the deaths of millions. Further damage would be wrought by the tidal waves, called tsunamis, reaching higher than 75 feet and traveling as fast as 400 miles per hour, that might deluge coastal areas and even submerge the whole of the Hawaiian Islands.

Aside from earthquakes and volcanoes, there is the real risk, seen every year, from hurricanes, floods, and famines. In 1992, Hurricane Andrew left a quarter of a million homeless and caused 46 billion dollars worth of damage. Far more destructive was the cyclone of 1970 that killed a million people in Bangladesh.

Floods, which are often a symptom of earthquakes and volcanic activity or other storms and unexpectedly harsh winters, can bring death, ruin, and disease. Some climatologists have also predicted the coming of another ice age or long-term dangers from the greenhouse effect. Still others fear the onset of a nuclear winter in which ash and debris—from a nuclear exchange or the eruptions of hundreds of volcanoes—hang in the atmosphere and choke off light and warmth, plunging the planet into perpetual darkness, the very same twilight foreseen by some seers.

Aside from Nostradamus, with his quatrains concerning earthquakes, famine, and drought, the chief prophets of global natural upheaval are Edgar Cayce and Gordon Michael Scallion. The Sleeping Prophet, Edgar Cayce, foretold of unprecedented earthquakes, with the disturbing assurance that New York, San Francisco, and Los Angeles will not be around by the end of the century. Scallion predicts that similar earthquakes will devastate portions of Europe and North America. Both Cayce and Scallion—along with the seer Lori Toye—have all drawn or inspired maps of the changed earth that will result from these disasters. Not surprisingly, the maps are generally similar, with coastal regions inundated, especially California and

New York, the Mississippi swelling to four times its present size, and the Great Lakes pouring into parts of the central states and midwest. Scallion, however, does not suggest to all who live in what he sees as danger zones that they flee. Rather, he is concerned more with personal development than trying to escape the coming deluge.

There shall be famine and war and earthquakes in diverse places. Snow and ice and great drought shall there be, and many dissensions among the people.

APOCALYPSE OF THOMAS

The sun in twenty degrees of Taurus [April 10], the earth shall
    shake so,
That the great theater will be filled and ruined
The sky, the air, and the earth shall be troubled in darkness
So that even unbelievers shall call upon God and the Saints.

NOSTRADAMUS IX, 83

In the coming 50 years an earthquake zone will develop in NE Pacific coast of Peru up through to the Arctic regions. Eastern cities of the U.S. will be affected, and parts of New York will be destroyed in 50-100 years. A series of earthquakes will cause the Azores to rise and Atlantis will resurface and be explored.

COUNT LOUIS HAMON (CHEIRO)

. . . water and fire will purify the Earth, and the time of true peace will commence.

PROPHECY OF MARY

❈

But slowly they are routed out
To seek diminishing water spout
And men will die of thirst before
The oceans rise to mount the shore.
And lands will crack and rend anew
You think it strange. It will come true.

MOTHER SHIPTON

❈

The great swarm of bees shall arise
But from where they come shall not be known
Beneath the vines the sentinel will be ambushed at night.
A city shall be betrayed by five tongues not naked.

NOSTRADAMUS IV, 26.

❈

There will be severe droughts in some parts of the planet and severe flooding in others. As a result of these, water will become as precious as gold owing to contamination from salt water and the changes in the water table. Summer and Spring will also become one long season in the United States.

GORDON MICHAEL SCALLION (ATTRIBUTED)

❈

❈

The second angel emptied his bowl over the sea, and it turned to blood, like the blood of a corpse, and every living creature in the sea died.

BOOK OF REVELATION

Red clouds like blood will pass in the sky, the crash of thunder will make the earth shake; lightning will flash through the streets . . . the ocean will cast itself over the land . . . the earth will be transformed into an immense cemetery.

MARIE JULIE JAHENNY DE LA FAUDAIS

On the day Gog attacks the land of Israel—it is the Lord Yahweh who speaks—I shall grow angry. In my anger, my jealousy, and the heat of my fury I say it: I swear that on that day there will be a fearful quaking in the land of Israel. At my presence the fish in the sea and the birds of heaven, the wild beasts and all the reptiles that crawl along the ground, and all men on the earth will quake. Mountains will fall, cliffs crumble, walls collapse . . .

BOOK OF EZEKIEL

Soon the Earth will shake and will tumble down and people will say, "Oh my God! Oh my God!" But the great Spirit will say, "They're not praying to me, they're saying 'All my Gold! All my Gold!'"

WALLACE BLACK ELK, LAKOTA SIOUX

A mighty wind will rise in the North sweeping heavy fog and densest dust by the command of God, and it will fill their throats and eyes so that they will be stricken with terror and shall cease their savagery.

ST. HILDEGARD OF BINGEN

The third angel emptied his bowl into the rivers and water springs and they turned into blood . . .

BOOK OF REVELATION

The earth will be broken up in many places. The early portion will see a change in the physical aspect of the west coast of America. There will be open waters appearing in the northern portions of Greenland. There will be new lands seen off the Caribbean Sea, and DRY land will appear . . . South America shall be shaken from the uppermost portion to the end, and in the Antarctic of Tierra del Fuego, LAND, and a strait with rushing waters.

EDGAR CAYCE

These are signs that great destruction is coming . . . You will hear of the sea turning black, and many living things dying because of it.

WHITE FEATHER (1958) OF THE HOPI BEAR CLAN,
RECORDED BY REV. DAVID YOUNG

Then will the earth tremble, and the sea bear no ships; heaven will not support the stars in their orbits, all voices of the Gods will be forced into silence; the fruits of the Earth will rot; the soil will turn barren, and the very air will sicken with sullen stagnation; all things will be disordered and awry, all good will disappear.

HERMES TRISMEGISTUS

The earth will undergo a long series of earthquakes and volcanic eruptions toward the end of the millennium. The volcanoes will bring a year of darkness along the Pacific Rim, and the greatest loss of life will come from the floods and other related effects of the upheavals rather than the events themselves.

GORDON MICHAEL SCALLION (ATTRIBUTED)

Having lifted the papers I had in my hand, I was struck by a phenomenon I had never seen before. The sun, which was fairly high, looked like a pale yellow opaque globe completely surrounded by a luminous halo, which nevertheless did not prevent me at all from staring attentively at the sun without the slightest discomfort. A very light cloud was before it. The opaque globe began moving outward, slowly turning over upon itself, and going from left to right and vice-versa. But within the globe very strong movements could be seen in all clarity and without interruption.

POPE PIUS XII

The whole country [of Scotland] will become so totally desolated and depopulated that the crow of a cock will not be heard, deer and other wild animals will be exterminated by a horrid black rain.

BRAHAN THE SEER

All public worship will be interrupted. A terrible and harsh famine will begin in the entire world and mainly in the western regions, such as has never taken place since the birth of the world.

JOÃO DE VATIGUERRO

See how Yahweh lays the earth waste, makes it a desert, buckles its surface, scatters its inhabitants . . . Ravaged, ravaged the earth will be, despoiled, despoiled, for Yahweh has uttered this word. The earth is mourning, pining away, the prick of earth's people are withering away. The earth is defiled by the feet of its inhabitants for they have transgressed the laws, violated the decree, broken the everlasting covenant.

BOOK OF ISAIAH

The sixth angel emptied his bowl over the great river Euphrates; all the water dried up so that a way was made for the kings of the East to come in . . .

BOOK OF REVELATION

The tides will rise beyond their ken
To bite away the shores and then
The mountains will begin to roar
And earthquakes split the plain to shore.
And flooding waters, rushing in
Will flood the lands with such a din
That mankind cowers in muddy fen
And snarls about his fellow men.
Man flees in terror from the floods
And kills, and rapes and lies in blood
And spilling blood by mankind's hands
Will stain and bitter many lands.

MOTHER SHIPTON

When the earth is shaken with her violent quaking and the earth brings forth her burdens, and man says: What has befallen her? On that day she shall tell her news, because your Lord had inspired her. On that day men shall come forth in sundry bodies that they may be shown their works. So, he who has done an atom's weight of good shall see it. And he who has done an atom's worth of evil shall see it.

QU'RAN

If we take precious things from the land we will perish.

HOPI PROPHECY

The peace among humanity which will set in after the great scourge [World War II] will only be a temporary peace. During this time the Earth will shake because of many concussions and convulsions. Humanity will endure continuous wars, which finally will lead to the last great war.

PROPHECY OF MARY AT FÁTIMA

Earth shattering, fire from the center of the earth
Shall bring an earthquake to the New City
For a long time shall two great rocks make war,
After that Arathusa [a legendary Greek nymph] shall color the river red.

NOSTRADAMUS I, 87

The whole country [of Scotland] will become so totally desolated and depopulated that the crow of a cock will not be heard, deer and other wild animals will be exterminated by a horrid black rain.

BRAHAN THE SEER

A great famine and pestilential wing
By a long rain shall come across the Arctic Pole
Samarobryn, a hundred leagues from the hemisphere
Shall live without law, exempt from politics.

NOSTRADAMUS VI, 5

For see how Yahweh comes in fire, his chariots like the whirlwind, to assuage his anger with burning his rebukes with flaming fire. For by fire will Yahweh execute fair judgment, and by his sword, on all people; and Yahweh's victims will be many.

BOOK OF ISAIAH

※

For forty years the rainbow shall not be seen
For forty years it shall be seen every day
The parched earth grows more dry
And a great flood when it shall appear.

NOSTRADAMUS I, 17

※

The day Gog attacks the land of Israel—declares the Lord Yahweh—my furious wrath will boil up. In my anger, in my jealousy, in the heat of my fury I say it: That day, I swear, there will be such a huge earthquake in the land of Israel, that the fish in the sea and the birds of heaven, the wild beasts, all the reptiles creeping along the ground, and all the people on the surface of the earth will quake before me. Mountains will fall, cliffs will crumble, all walls collapse, and I shall summon every kind of sword against him . . . I shall punish him with plague and bloodshed, and rain down torrential rain, hailstorms, fire, and brimstone on him, on his troops and on the many nations with him.

BOOK OF DANIEL

※

※

A world destruction as happened to Atlantis 11,000 years ago . . .
instead of Atlantis all of England and parts of NW European coast
will sink into the sea, in contrast, the sunken Azores region, the Isle
of Poseidonis, will again be raised from the sea.

MADAME HELENA BLAVATSKY

A cracking, the earth cracks open, a jolting, the earth gives a
jolt, a lurching, the earth lurches backwards and forwards. The
earth will reel to and fro like a drunkard, it will be shaken like a
shanty; so heavy will be its sin on it, it will fall, never to rise
again.

BOOK OF ISAIAH

The first blow of the sword of God will fall like lightning upon
humanity. The mountain and all nature shall shake because of the
disorder and the misdeeds of men.

MARY AT LA SALETTE

In the year that Saturn and Mars shall be fiery,
The air shall be very dry, a great meteor
From secret fires the great place burns without heat
There shall be little rain, hot winds, wars, and attacks.

NOSTRADAMUS IV, 67

From now on tidal waves and cyclones will bring enormous destruction.

COUNT LOUIS HAMON (CHEIRO)

The sea will heave itself beyond its bounds engulfing mighty cities.

BRIGHAM YOUNG

The seventh angel emptied his bowl into the air, and a great voice shouted from the sanctuary, "The end has come." Then there were flashes of lightning and peals of thunder and the most violent earthquake, *that anyone has ever seen since there have been men on the earth* . . . Every island vanished and the mountains disappeared; and hail, with great hailstones weighing a talent each, fell from the sky on people.

BOOK OF REVELATION

. . . the glacial age will by degrees be repeated in Northern Europe; such countries as Ireland, Great Britain, Sweden, Norway, Denmark, the north parts of Russia, Germany, France, and Spain, will gradually become uninhabitable. This alteration will be compensated for by the development of a temperate climate affecting such countries as China, India, Africa, and Egypt, and in consequence a rapid increase of civilization will be the result in all these countries.

COUNT LOUIS HAMON (CHEIRO)

Not every land on earth will sink
But these will wallow in stench and stink
Of rotting bodies of beast and man
Of vegetation crisped on land.

MOTHER SHIPTON

❊

Garden of the World, near the New City
In the road of the hollowed mountains
Shall be taken and hurled into a pitch
And forced to drink water poisoned with sulfur.

NOSTRADAMUS X, 49

❊

There will be upheavals in the Arctic and the Antarctic that will
make for the eruptions of volcanoes in the Torrid areas and there
will be shifting then of the poles—so that where there have been
those of frigid or semi-tropical will become the most tropical and
moss and ferns will grow . . .

EDGAR CAYCE

❊

Balance will be upset and terrible forces shall be unleashed when
pieces of the Moon are returned to the Earth.

HOPI PROPHECY

❊

❊

Blow the ram's-horn in Zion, sound the alarm on my holy
mountain! Let everybody in the country tremble, for the Day of
Yahweh is coming, yes it is near. Day of darkness and gloom, Day
of cloud and blackness. Like the dawn, across the mountains spreads
a vast and mighty people, such as has never been before, such as will
never be again to the remotest ages.

BOOK OF JOEL

A period of natural convulsions during which a large portion of the
human race will perish. Earthquakes of great severity, enormous
tidal waves would seem to be the agents. War appears only in the
early stages and appears to be a signal for the crisis to follow. The
crisis will come in an instant. The destruction and dislocation of
civilized life will be beyond belief. There will be a short period of
chaos followed by some reconstruction; the total period of
upheavals will be roughly three years. The chief centers of
disturbance will be the Eastern Mediterranean basin, where not less
than five countries will entirely disappear. Also in the Atlantic
there will be a rise of land which will be a cause of those waves
which will bring about great disasters upon the Americans, the
Irish and Western European shore, involving all of the low-lying
British coasts. There are indicated further great upheavals in the
southern Pacific and in the Japanese region. Mankind can be saved
by returning to its spiritual values.

SIR ARTHUR CONAN DOYLE

The great famine I see approaching
Shall turn from one place to another before becoming world-wide
So great and terrible shall it be that they come to pluck
The roots from the trees and the child from the breast.

NOSTRADAMUS I, 67

❖

The earthquake shall come in the month of May
Saturn in Capricorn, Jupiter and Mercury in Taurus
Venus in Cancer, Mars in Virgo
Then hail shall fall bigger than an egg.

NOSTRADAMUS X, 67

❖

The changes of season shall produce only half their verdure.

ST. COLUMBKILLE

❖

Many portions of the east coast will be disturbed, as well as in the
Pacific. And what is the coast line now of many a land will be the
bed of the ocean. Even many of the battlefields of the present (1944-
1945) will be ocean . . . Portions of the now east coast of New York,
or New York City itself, will in the main disappear. This will be
another generation, though, here, while the southern portions of
Carolina, Georgia, these will disappear.

EDGAR CAYCE

❖

❖

The white men will battle against other peoples on other lands—
with those who possessed the first light of wisdom. Terrible will be
the result.

WHITE FEATHER (1958) OF THE HOPI BEAR CLAN,
RECORDED BY REV. DAVID YOUNG

Immediately, there was a violent earthquake, and a tenth of the city
collapsed; seven thousand persons were killed in the earthquake, and
the survivors, overcome with fear, could only praise the God of
heaven.

BOOK OF REVELATION

It is said that the oceans will entirely flood certain parts of the earth,
and that from moment to moment millions of men will perish.

PROPHECY OF MARY AT FÁTIMA

There will be earthquakes and signs in the sun. Toward the end,
darkness will cover the earth. When everyone believes that peace is
assured, when everyone least expects it, the great happening will
begin. Revolution will break out in Italy almost at the same time as
in France. For some time the Church will be without a Pope.

THE ECSTATIC OF TOURS

In the next few years lands will appear in the Atlantic as well as in the Pacific.

EDGAR CAYCE

❌

An Astrological Disaster

The King of Prophets, Nostradamus, was one of history's most accomplished astrologers, filling his prophetic quatrains with astrological references and obvious calculations from his long acquaintance with planetary alignments and the movement of the celestial realm. It is likely, then, that Nostradamus saw cataclysms for the end of the twentieth century precisely because of the astrological events that were calculated even in the sixteenth century and that cause alarm to modern-day astrologers. The two most serious happenings are the Grand Cross of 1999 and the Grand Alignment of 2000. Both alignments are considered by some astrologers to pose a genuine threat to bring planet-wide calamities, perhaps even the end of life on earth.

The first alignment, occurring on August 18, 1999, will be preceded on August 11 by the last eclipse of the millennium (itself seen as quite ill-favored) and will bring the planets into a rare series of placements, astrologically speaking. The Moon and Mars will be in Scorpio; the Sun, Mercury, and Venus will be in Leo; Jupiter and Saturn will be in Taurus; Uranus and Neptune will be in Aquarius; and Pluto will be close to Sagittarius. It is pointed out that the four planets are placed (or

❌

quartered) in signs traditionally symbolized by the four beasts of the Book of Revelation, the Beasts of the Apocalypse: Leo the Lion, Scorpio the Eagle; Taurus the Bull; and Aquarius the Water Bearer, or the Winged Man. What exactly is supposed to take place? If the "experts" are right, the Grand Cross formed by the unusual alignment will release frightful energies, setting off severe storms, flooding, and tectonic activity. For proof of this, one can observe the fruits of a similar, albeit milder, Grand Cross that was formed in March 1993, followed by the worst winter of the century and ruinous flooding along the Mississippi.

Even bigger than the Grand Cross will be the Grand Alignment of May 4, 2000, during which the Earth will be accompanied only by Pluto on one side of the Sun, opposed on the other side by Venus, Mercury, Jupiter, Saturn, and the Moon; Uranus and Neptune will rest midway between the groups. This does not sound too dreadful to the average reader, but to students of astrology, the planets in opposition could cause a gravitational pull on the Sun and the Earth. The Sun could be troubled by sunspots, felt here on the planet through colossal weather changes and earthquakes. The Earth itself could be affected in much the same way as the Sun, being pulled by the gravitational equivalent of another moon in the sky. Such a sudden pull might bring tidal changes, floods, earthquakes, and perhaps the shifting of the planet's axis, with genuinely dire consequences for humanity as the Alps, Andes, Rockies, and Himalayas become, in a matter of hours, very expensive beach-front property.

Trouble for those who are waiting so longingly for the Day of Yahweh! What will the Day of Yahweh mean for you? It will mean darkness, not light, as when a man escapes a lion's mouth, only to meet a bear; he enters his house and puts his hand on the wall only for a snake to bite him. Will not the Day of Yahweh be darkness, not light? It will all be gloom, without a single ray of light.

BOOK OF AMOS

When there is the first breaking up of some conditions in the South Sea and those as apparent in the sinking and rising of that almost opposite the same or in the Mediterranean and the Etna area. Then we will know it has begun.

EDGAR CAYCE

By a flood and the great pestilence
The great city shall be attacked
The sentinel and guard shall be surprised
Captured suddenly, but none shall be hurt.

NOSTRADAMUS IX, 82

. . . nature will tremble because of the chaos and misdeeds of humanity, which will rise up to the heavens.

PROPHECY OF MARY AT LA SALETTE

PROPHECIES: 2000

Yet greater sign there be to see
As man nears latter century
Three sleeping mountains gather breath
And spew out mud, and ice and death.
And earthquakes swallow town and town,
In lands as yet to me unknown.

MOTHER SHIPTON

�֍

. . . the elements of all the world shall be desolate; air, earth, sea,
burning fire, and sky and night, all days unite into one fire, and to
one arid, shapeless mass to come.

SIBYLLINE ORACLES

✖

. . . the southern coast of California—and the area between Salt
Lake and southern portion of Nevada—may expect, within three
months following some inundation by the earthquakes.

EDGAR CAYCE

✖

The great maritime city of the ocean
Surrounded by a marsh of crystal
In the winter solstice and in the spring
Will be tested by a terrible wind.

NOSTRADAMUS IX, 48

✖

✖

. . . Europe will be covered by a yellow fog. The cattle in the fields will die from this yellow fog . . . Famine will annihilate those who remain, so that Europe will be too large.

COUNTESS FRANCESCA DE BILLIANTE

❊

. . . famine shall strike and fishes shall forsake the rivers.

ST. COLUMBKILLE

❊

Alas! What great loss shall learning endure,
Before the completion of the cycle of the moon,
By fire, great flood, and ignorant rulers
More than a long age before it can be made restored.

NOSTRADAMUS I, 62

❊

The sun and the moon fighting one with the other, a continuous rolling and noise of thunder and lightning, thunder and earthquake; cities falling and men perishing in their overthrow, a continual dearth for lack of rain, a terrible pestilence and great mortality, mighty and untimely, so they that die lack burial: and the bearing forth of brethren and sisters and kinsmen shall be upon one bier.

APOCALYPSE OF THOMAS

❊

❊

That the periodical sinking and reappearance of mighty continents, now called Atlantean and Lemurian by modern writers, is not fiction will be demonstrated. It is only in the 20th century that portions, if not the whole, of the present work will be vindicated.

MADAME HELENA BLAVATSKY

In the Cyclades, in Perinthus and Larissa
And in Sparta and the whole of the Peloponnesus
A great famine, and a great plague
Lasting nine months in the whole peninsula.

NOSTRADAMUS V, 90

And it shall come to pass that whosoever gets safe out of the war shall die in the earthquake and whosoever gets safe out of the earthquake shall be burned by the fire, and whosoever gets safe out of the fire shall be destroyed by famine.

BOOK OF BARUCH

Through the heat of the sun upon the sea,
At Negrepont shall the fish be half-boiled
The inhabitants shall come to eat them,
While in Rhodes and Genoa there is starvation.

NOSTRADAMUS II, 3

When in the world there shall appear quakings of places, tumult of peoples, schemings of nations, confusion of leaders, disquietude of princes, then shall you understand that it is of these things the Most High has spoken since the days that were aforetime from the beginning.

BOOK OF EZEKIEL

The earth will be broken up in the western portion of America. The greater portion of Japan must go into the sea. The upper portion of Europe will be changed as in the twinkle of an eye.

EDGAR CAYCE

God said: "First I will make an earthquake for the fall of four-footed beasts and of men; and when you see that brother gives up brother to death, and that children shall rise up against their parents, and that a woman forsakes her own husband, and when nation shall rise up against nation in war. Then you will know that the end is near."

REVELATION TO ESDRAS

The trees shall not bear the usual quantity of fruit, fisheries shall become unproductive, and the earth shall not yield its abundance.

ST. COLUMBKILLE

A child shall be born with two teeth in his mouth.
Stones shall fall like rain upon Tuscany
A few years later there shall be neither wheat nor barley.
To feed those who shall faint from hunger.

NOSTRADAMUS III, 42

Los Angeles, San Francisco, most of all these will be destroyed
before New York even.

EDGAR CAYCE

On the mountains of Bailly and la Bresle
Shall be concealed the fierce people of Grenoble
Beyond Lyons, Vienne, there shall fall a hail
And locust on the earth so that not a third remains.

NOSTRADAMUS IX, 69

Wars and Armageddon

A great lament will come over all mankind and only a small number will survive the tempest, the pestilence, and the horror.

PASTOR BARTHOLOMAEUS

As those who fought in the Gulf War of 1991 are able to attest, the post-Cold War world—the time of the so-called New World Order—has proven far more complicated than many had imagined. As the year 2000 approaches, the geopolitical stability of the last decade has been replaced by a series of global hot spots that threaten to spill over and spark serious, even worldwide, wars and suffering. For example, there are the troubles found in the Korean Peninsula, where the leader there, Kim Il Jong, rules with an iron fist and harbors ambitions of solving North Korea's mounting economic and social troubles by conquering South Korea. There are also the traditionally troubled areas of India and Pakistan (an ever-looming crisis made all the more disturbing by the possession by both sides of nuclear weapons); the Balkans; and of course, the Holy Land, the scene of so many wars since the founding of Israel in 1948.

Of these the most likely and most potentially catastrophic is that of the Arab-Israeli conflict. With the region still recovering from the Gulf War and with the very real possibility of the use of chemical, bacteriological, and nuclear weapons by the combatants, a renewed Middle East war could involve the United States, Russia, China, and the countries of the Mediterranean and Near East, as well as possibly launching a global *jihad*, or holy war, should Islamic holy sites, such as the Dome of the Rock or Mecca, be damaged or wiped out in the fighting.

Aside from those traditional sources of conflict around the globe, there are other potential causes of war looming on the horizon. Droughts in China, the Near East, and the Middle East could bring starvation, water shortages, political and economic instability, and bitter hostilities over dwindling natural resources. Economic hardships—such as another global depression or the much anticipated deflationary recession—could force nation against nation. Plagues might reduce once-thriving cities to wastelands, beset by chaos and a breakdown of all stability the likes of which has not been seen since the worst days of the Black Death.

Unfortunately, prophets have seen more about wars for the coming years than about virtually any other endeavor. The Old and New Testaments contain two of the most disturbing sources for prophecies on the dangers of the coming wars. First, there is the Book of Revelation, in the New Testament, with its foretelling of the angels pouring out bowls of inexpressible misery upon the face of the earth. Second, there is Ezekiel, with its account of the infamous Gog and Magog waging war upon Israel. Gog and Magog's attack is connected by some interpreters to the Antichrist, the Apocalypse, and the climactic Battle of Armageddon, to be fought in the valley of Megiddo, in Israel. The final struggle between good and evil, the Battle of Armageddon will leave the whole region soaked in the blood of uncounted dead. That war is coming before the millennium, perhaps the final and feared Third World War (starting unexpectedly and soon engulfing the globe), is attested by prophets from across the ages, including Nostradamus, Stormberger, and Mother Shipton.

. . . a war shall come, before which all previous wars shall fade. Streams of fire will come forth from clouds, where there are no clouds . . . all chief cities on both sides of the ocean will be buried beneath rubble and ashes, and it will be cause for great wailing. The horrors of war will be also on and over the water, and the enemy will be smitten on the head with much loss, and tears will flow and much blood, and then all will be ended.

PROPHECY OF MARIENTHAL

After the second great struggle between the nations will come a third universal conflagration, which will decide everything. There will be entirely new weapons. In one day more men will perish than in all the previous wars together. Battles will be fought with artificial weapons. Enormous catastrophes will take place. The nations of the Earth will enter into these calamities with open eyes. They shall not be aware of what is taking place, and those who will know and speak will be silenced. All will be different than before, and in many places the Earth will be a great cemetery. The third great war will be the end of many nations.

STORMBERGER

Cobwebs shall be spun across the sky near the Day of the Great Purification.

HOPI PROPHECY

In the year that the great seventh is completed [2000]
There shall occur at the time of slaughter
Not far from the start of the grand millennium
The dead shall rise from their graves.

NOSTRADAMUS X, 74

You will hear of wars and reports of wars; see that you are not
alarmed, for these things must happen, but it will not yet be the end.
Nation will rise against nation, and kingdom against kingdom; there
will be famines and earthquakes from place to place. All these things
are the beginnings of the labor pains.

THE GOSPEL OF MATTHEW

Tears, cries and howlings of complaint
An inhuman heart, cruel, dark, and cold.
Lake Geneva, the islands, those of Genoa
Blood spilled, the bells ring, and no mercy is given.

NOSTRADAMUS VI, 81

Mourn, mourn for this great city,
Babylon, so powerful a city,
doomed as you are within a single hour.

BOOK OF REVELATION

. . . all the earth will be in a state of tumult. The time of "nation fighting against nation" will take place after the birth of the Antichrist. Then the world shall be stripped of its beauty through the destruction of humanity.

LACTANTIUS

Against the reds shall unite sects
Fire, water, iron, rope, weakened by peace
Those who conspire shall be put to death
Save for one who, above all, shall ruin the world.

NOSTRADAMUS IX, 51

It will be possible to carve up the heavens with swords.

PASTOR BARTHOLOMAEUS

Others scorched by the fire ran hither and yon,
As in the midst of a forest conflagration,
The steeds . . . and the chariots also,
Burnt by the energy of that weapon . . .
Looked like the tops of trees
Burnt in a forest fire . . .

MAHABHARATA

Twice risen up and twice defeated
The East will also wear down the West
After many struggles the adversary
By the sea expelled shall fail in need.

NOSTRADAMUS VIII, 59

❈

To make hearts sink and make sure many fall, I have posted the slaughtering sword at every gate to flash like lightning polished for slaughter.

THE BOOK OF EZEKIEL

❈

It is only War in the end that will save humanity. It is only when the world will be satiated with blood, destruction, and violence, that it will wake from its present nightmare of madness—and thus it is that the coming "War of Wars" fits into the design of things.

COUNT LOUIS HAMON (CHEIRO)

❈

. . . that time will arise which brings affliction; for it shall come and pass by with quick vehemence, and it shall be turbulent coming in the heat of indignation. And it shall come to pass in those days that all the inhabitants of the earth will be moved one against the other, because they know not that My judgment has drawn nigh.

BOOK OF BARUCH

❈

❈

About times and dates, brothers, there is no need to write to you for you are well aware in any case that the Day of the Lord is going to come like a thief in the night. It is when people are saying, "How quiet and peaceful it is" that sudden destruction falls on them, as suddenly as labor pains come on a pregnant woman, and there is no escape.

1 THESSALONIANS

Then I saw the beast, with all the kings of the earth and their armies, gathered together to fight the Rider and his army. But the beast was taken prisoner, together with the false prophet who had worked miracles on the beast's behalf and by them had deceived all who had been branded with the mark of the beast and worshiped his statue. These two were thrown alive into the fiery lake of burning sulphur.

BOOK OF REVELATION

The chastisement will come when carriages go without horses and many accidents fill the world with woe. It will come when thoughts are flying around the earth in the twinkling of an eye, when long tunnels are made for horseless machines, when men can fly in the air and ride under the sea, when ships are wholly made of metal, when fire and water great marvels do, when even the poor can read books, and when many taxes are levied for war.

MOTHER SHIPTON

In the 20th century there will be wars and fury that will last a long time; whole provinces shall be emptied of their inhabitants, and kingdoms shall be thrown into confusion. In many places the land shall be left untilled, and there shall be great slaughters of the upper class. The right hand of the world shall fear the left, and the north shall prevail over the south.

BISHOP CHRISTIANOS AGEDA

Leave, leave, depart Geneva all
Saturn will transform iron from gold
The opposite of the positive ray shall slay all
The sky will give signs before the event.

NOSTRADAMUS IX, 44

. . . Son of man, turn towards Gog, to the country of Magog, towards the paramount prince of Meshech and Tubal, and prophecy against him. Say, "The Lord Yahweh says this: I am against you, Gog, paramount prince of Meshech and Tubal. I shall turn you about, I shall fix hooks in your jaws and bring you out with your entire army, horses and horsemen, all perfectly equipped, a huge array armed with shields and bucklers and all wielding swords. Persia and Cush and Put are with them, all with buckles and helmet; Gomer and its troops, Beth-Togarmah in the far north and all its troops and many nations with you."

BOOK OF EZEKIEL

When pictures look alive, with movement free,
When ships like fish swim beneath the sea,
When man outstripping birds can soar the sky,
Then half the world deep drenched in blood shall die.

TOMBSTONE INSCRIPTION, KIRBY CEMETERY,
ESSEX ENGLAND, 17TH CENTURY

The populous places shall become uninhabitable,
Terrible disagreement over lands
Kingdoms bestowed upon men incapable of prudence
The three brothers shall suffer death and dissension.

NOSTRADAMUS II, 95

The machine of flying fire
Shall come to trouble the besieged leader.
Within shall be such rioting
That the forgotten will be in despair.

NOSTRADAMUS VI, 34

The Arab prince, Mars, Sol, Venus, Leo
The rule of the Church will be overcome by sea
Towards Persia, nearly a million men
Shall invade Egypt, the true serpent, and Byzantium.

NOSTRADAMUS V, 25

PROPHECIES: 2000

The Battles of the past will only be skirmishes compared to the battles that will occur. All nations of the Earth will fight each other . . . The warriors shall rise up in the heavens to take the stars and hurl them on the cities, to set fire to buildings and cause enormous destruction.

St. Odilia

***

(It was) a single projectile
Charged with all the power of the Universe.
An incandescent column of smoke and flame
As bright as 10,000 suns
Rose in all its splendor . . .

Mahabharata

***

From Fez shall the kingdom stretch out to Europe
The city destroyed by fire and sword
The great one of Asia, by land and sea, with a vast army
So that blue, greens, he will drive the crosses to death.

Nostradamus VI, 80

***

In those years and days shall war be kindled upon war, the four ends of the earth shall be in commotion and fight against each other. Thereafter shall be quakings of clouds, darkness, and death, and persecutions of them that believe in me and against the elect.

Apocalypse of Thomas

***

***

When the close of times draws near, a great prophet shall be sent from God to turn men to the knowledge of the Lord . . . Wherever men shall not hear him, he will shut up the heavens and cause it to withhold its rains; he will turn their water into blood, and torment them with thirst and hunger . . .

LACTANTIUS

. . . it shall seem, from the kingdoms spoiled those of the East, that God has freed Satan from his infernal incarceration to cause to be born Gog and Magog, who shall make so great and abominable a breach in the Churches, that neither the reds nor the whites . . . shall not judge of it . . .

NOSTRADAMUS, EPISTLE TO KING HENRY II OF FRANCE

There will be poisonous clouds, and rays which burn more deeply than the sun on the equator; armies will march encased in iron; flying ships full of dreadful bombs and arrows, and flying stars with sulfuric fire which exterminate entire cities in an instant.

PROPHECY OF WARSAW

The sky shall burn at forty-five degrees
Fire nears the great New City
In moments, scattered flames shall erupt.

NOSTRADAMUS VI, 97

38

And when those things which were predicted come to pass, then shall confusion fall upon all men, and some of them shall fall in battle, and some of them shall perish in anguish, and some of them shall be destroyed by their own. Then the Most High will reveal those peoples whom He has prepared before, and they shall come and make war with the leader.

BOOK OF BARUCH

As foreshadowed in Ezekiel, Chapter 38, the great battle of Armageddon will be fought on the plains of Palestine. It is clearly set out for all those who may choose to read that this conflict will be a life and death struggle for the contending armies fighting in Palestine.

COUNT LOUIS HAMON (CHEIRO)

Human pride will lower its eyes, human arrogance will be humbled, and Yahweh alone will be exalted, on that day. That will be a day for Yahweh Sabaoth, for all who are majestic and haughty, for all who are proud, to be brought low, for all the cedars of Lebanon, high and proud, and for all the oaks of Bashan; for all the high mountains and for all the proud hills; for every lofty tower and for every towering wall; for all the ships of Tarshish and for everything held precious. Human pride will be humbled, human arrogance brought low, and Yahweh alone will be exalted on that day.

BOOK OF ISAIAH

Those who were at ease will be suppressed suddenly
The world shall be put into trouble by three brothers
The maritime city will be seized by its enemies
Hunger, fire, blood, plague, and a double of all evils.

NOSTRADAMUS VIII, 17

When sin and righteousness, blasphemy and violence and all kinds
of deeds increase, an apostasy in transgression and uncleanness
increase, a great chastisement shall come from heaven.

BOOK OF ENOCH

A great King captured by the hands of a young one
Not far from Easter, confusion, of a blade
When the lightning is at the top of the mast, a captive eternal
Three brothers will be wounded and murdered.

NOSTRADAMUS IX, 36

A single day will see the burial of mankind, all that the long
forebearance of fortune has produced, all that has been brought to
eminence, all that is well-known and all that is beautiful; mighty
thrones, great nations—all will sink into one abyss, all will be
toppled in one hour.

SIBYLLINE ORACLES

... Then (the god of that mighty weapon)
Bore away crowds of Samsaptakas
With steeds and elephants and cars and weapons,
As if these were dry leaves of trees ...
Borne away by the wind, O King,
They looked highly beautiful
Like flying away from trees ...

MAHABHARATA

❇

When those of the Northern Pole are united together
There will be much fear and dread in the East
One newly elected aided by those who tremble
Rhodes, Byzantium shall be covered in barbarous blood.

NOSTRADAMUS VI, 21

❇

Yet now you have abandoned and humiliated us,
you no longer take the field with our armies,
you leave us to fall back before the enemy,
those who hate us plunder us at will.
You hand us over like sheep for slaughter,
you scatter us among the nations,
you sell your people for a trifle
and make no profit for the sale.

BOOK OF PSALMS

❇

❇

When weapons and letter are encased in a fish of iron,
He shall go out of it who will make war
His well prepared fleet by the sea
Appears by the Latin shore.

NOSTRADAMUS II, 5

These states will lock in fiercest strife
And seek to take each other's life.
When North shall thus divide the south
And Eagle build in Lions mouth
Then tax and blood and cruel war
Shall come to every humble door.

MOTHER SHIPTON

In the last terrible desolation of the world, the final High Priest of
the True God shall reign. Criminal Rome will be destroyed and the
terrible judge, in his Glory, will judge all nations.

MONK OF PADUA

Mars and the scepter [Jupiter] will be in conjunction [2002]
Under Cancer a calamitous war.
Soon after a new ruler will be anointed
Who shall bring peace to the world for a long time.

NOSTRADAMUS VI, 24

On the Day of Yahweh's anger, by the fire of his jealousy, the whole earth will be consumed. For he will destroy, yes, annihilate everyone living on earth.

BOOK OF ZEPHENIAH

It may be that revolutions and upheavals we see around us on all sides may for the time being bring about the fall of Empires, the destruction of thrones, the death of the "old" and the birth of the "new."

COUNT LOUIS HAMON (CHEIRO)

In the climate opposite to Babylon,
There shall be a terrible spilling of blood.
On land, sea, and in the air shall Heaven seem unjust
Sects, famines, kingdoms, pestilence, and confusion.

NOSTRADAMUS I, 55

Oh! The dragon has appeared in all countries and has brought terrible confusion everywhere. There is war everywhere. Men and people have risen up one against the other. War, war, war—civil war and foreign war . . . Everything is mourning and death; famine reigns in the fields.

PROPHECY OF PREMOL

After a few hours
All foodstuffs were infected . . .
. . . To escape from this fire
The soldiers threw themselves in streams
To wash themselves and their equipment . . .

MAHABHARATA

❈

The supposed union will last only a short time
Some shall be changed, others briefly reformed
In ships people will be imprisoned
When Rome has a new Leopard.

NOSTRADAMUS VI, 20

❈

Fire from the sky to the earth, the color of gold shall be seen
Struck of the high born one, a marvelous event.
Great massacre of humanity, a nephew seized from the great one;
The proud one escapes as the dead look on.

NOSTRADAMUS II, 92

❈

Strife will arise through the period . . . Watch for them in Libya and
in Egypt, and in Syria. Through the straits around these areas above
Australia; in the Indian Ocean and the Persian Gulf . . .

EDGAR CAYCE

❈

❈

I shall gather all the nations to Jerusalem for battle. The city will be taken, the horses plundered, the women ravished. Half the city will go into exile, but the rest of the people will not be ejected from the city. Then Yahweh will sally out and fight those nations as once he fought on the day of battle.

Book of Zechariah

The twentieth century will bring death and destruction, apostasy from the Church, discord in families, cities, and governments; it will be a century of three great wars with intervals of only a few decades. They will grow even more devastating and bloody and cast into ruin not only Germany, but finally all nations, East and West.

The Prophecy of Maria Laach Monastery

Nothing will be anymore holy. Everything will be upset. The great clearance will begin. All nations will be pitted against each other. The free life and thought will be exiled and imprisoned. Seven leaders will rule and will try to get everything under discipline. It will be a dreadful time.

Stormberger

Mankind must prepare itself for sufferings such as it has never before experienced.

Pope Pius XII

A great change shall come to pass, such as no mortal man will have anticipated. This struggle is the confrontation between Heaven and Hell. Old states shall die and light and dark will be matched against each other with swords, but it will be the swords of a different kind. It will be possible to carve up the heavens with these swords. A great lament will come over all mankind and only a small number will survive the tempest, the pestilence, and the horror.

PASTOR BARTHOLOMAEUS

The gods will make it seem to humanity
That they are the authors of a great war
The once quiet sky shall show weapons and rockets
The greater damage shall occur on the left.

NOSTRADAMUS I, 91

Awake, sword, against my shepherd, against the man who is close to me—declares Yahweh Sabaoth! Strike the shepherd, scatter the sheep! And I shall turn my hand against the young! So will it be, throughout the country—declares Yahweh Sabaoth—two-thirds in it will be cut off (be killed) and the other third will be left. I shall pass this third through the fire, refine them as silver is refined, test them as gold is tested.

BOOK OF ZECHARIAH

And Christian one fights Christian two
And nations sigh, yet nothing do
And yellow men great power gain
From mighty bear with whom they've lain.

MOTHER SHIPTON

In all parts of the world there will be wars and revolutions, and much blood will be spilled. Distress, disasters, and poverty will everywhere be great, since pestilential maladies, scarcity, and other misfortunes will follow one another.

BISHOP GEORGE MICHAEL WITTMANN

I come to reconcile all people, to seek them out, to give them faith, which has disappeared in the noise and din of an atomic awakening which is at the point of bursting out. My message is of faith, love and hope. More than anything, it brings reconciliation between people and nations. It is the only thing that can save this century from war and eternal death . . . If a change does not come and a conversion of life, one will perish under the fire, war and death.

PROPHECY OF MARY AT FÁTIMA

Wars and miracles will occur until the people believe in Christ— toward the end of the world.

ST. THOMAS BECKET

The two shall not for long remain allies.
Within thirteen years they surrender to the barbarian Satrap
There will be such loss on both sides
That one shall bless the Bark [of Peter] and its master.

NOSTRADAMUS V, 78

✖

. . . A shaft fatal as the rod of death.
It measured three cubes and six feet . . .
It was destructive of all living creatures . . .

MAHABHARATA

✖

Within a short time, after not a long interval
By land and sea shall a mighty tumult be made,
The naval battle shall be greater than ever
Fire and beasts shall make further tumult.

NOSTRADAMUS II, 40

✖

Soon before the setting of the Sun, a battle shall be engaged
The great people shall be in doubt
The seaport overcome, it makes no answer
The bridge and the sepulcher shall be in strange lands.

NOSTRADAMUS I, 37

✖

✖

Behold! The days come, and it shall be when the time of the age ripened, and the harvest of its evil and good seeds has come, that the Mighty One will bring upon the earth and its inhabitants and upon its rulers perturbation of spirit and stupor of heart. And they shall hate one another . . .

THE BOOK OF BARUCH

The great Day of Yahweh is near, near, and coming with great speed. How bitter the sound of the Day of Yahweh, the Day when the warrior shouts his cry of war. That Day is a day of retribution, a day of distress and tribulation, a day of ruin and devastation, a day of darkness and gloom, a day of cloud and thick fog, a day of trumpet blast and battle cry against fortified town and high corner tower.

BOOK OF ZEPHANIAH

The world will be harassed by civil wars and greater destruction than ever before. Germany will be partitioned and have many enemies. Religion will be greatly oppressed and monks will be banished. During this oppression, the Cross will shine forth in double splendor through many nations because of the mighty ruler, to the astonishment of all.

FATHER LAVINSKY

THE FOUR HORSEMEN OF THE APOCALYPSE

Then I saw the lamb break one of the seven seals, and I heard one of the four animals shout in a voice like thunder, "Come!" Immediately a white horse appeared, and the rider on it was holding a bow; he was given the victor's crown and he went away, to go from victory to victory.

When he broke the second seal, I heard the second living creature shout, "Come!" And out came another horse, bright red, and its rider was given this duty: to take away peace from the earth and set people killing each other. He was given a huge sword.

When he broke the third seal, I heard the third living creature shout, "Come!" Immediately I saw a black horse appear, and its rider was holding a pair of scales; and I seemed to hear a voice shout from among the four animals and say, "A ration of corn for a day's wages, and three rations of barley for a day's wages, but do not tamper with the oil or the wine."

When he broke the fourth seal, I heard the voice of the fourth animal shout, "Come!" Immediately another horse appeared, deathly pale, and its rider was called Plague, and Hades followed at its heels.

They were given authority over a quarter of the earth, to kill by the sword, by famine, by plague and wild beasts.

REVELATION (6:1-8)

When men fly like birds, ten great kings will go to war against each other, and the universe will be under arms.

JAPANESE PROPHECY

⬗⬖

... The corpses were so burned
As to be unrecognizable.
Their hair and nails fell out;
Pottery broke without apparent cause.
And the birds turned white.

MAHABHARATA

⬗⬖

The great city will soon be abandoned
Not one inhabitant will be left.
Wall, sex, church and virgin violated
By sword, fire, plague, cannon shall people be slain.

NOSTRADAMUS III, 84

⬗⬖

The sword, the sword has been sharpened and polished. Sharpened for slaughter, polished to flash like lightning ... He has had it polished to be wielded, their sword sharpened and polished to be put in the slaughterer's hand! Shout and wail, son of man, for it will come on my people ...

BOOK OF EZEKIEL

⬗⬖

⬗⬖

51

Return and rebuild Jerusalem to the coming of an Anointed prince, seven weeks and sixty-two weeks, with squares and ramparts restored and rebuilt but in a time of trouble. And after the sixty-two weeks an Anointed One put to death without his . . . city and sanctuary ruined by a prince who is to come. The end of that prince will be catastrophe and, until the end, there will be war and all the devastation decreed. He will strike a firm alliance with many people for the space of a week; and for the space of one half-week he will put a stop to sacrifice and oblation, and on the wing of the temple will be appalling abominations until the end, until the doom assigned to the devastation.

BOOK OF DANIEL

※

With Sagittarius at its ascendant
A pond shall be stricken by the scythe.
Plague, famine, death from martial hand;
The Century approaches its renewal.

NOSTRADAMUS I, 16

※

For those who live the century through
In fear and trembling this shall do.
Flee to the mountains and the dens
To bog and forest and wild fens.

MOTHER SHIPTON

※

※

The mastery left to two, they shall not keep it for long,
They shall go to war after three years and seven months,
The two vestals shall rise up against them.
The victor shall be born on the soil of America.

NOSTRADAMUS IV, 95

In the latter days there will be great wars and bloodshed. The fury of the wars will endure for a long time. Whole provinces will be left naked, and uninhabited, many cities forsaken of people, the nobility slaughtered . . .

BLESSED JOHANNES AMADEUS DE SYLVA

An unusual chastisement of the human race will take place toward the end of the world.

BLESSED MARIA DE AGREDA

. . . So powerful that it could destroy
The earth in an instant—
A great soaring sound in smoke and flames . . .
And on it sits Death . . .

MAHABHARATA

Hence the time comes for the End, the king of the south will try conclusions with him; but the king of the north will come storming down on him with chariots, cavalry, and a large fleet. He will invade countries, overrun them and drive on. He will invade the Land of Splendor, and many will fall . . . he will reach out to attack countries: Egypt will not escape him. The gold and silver treasures and all the valuables of Egypt will lie in his power. Libyans and Cushites will be at his feet: but reports coming from the East and the North will worry him, and in a great fury he will set out to bring ruin and complete destruction to many. He will pitch tents of his royal headquarters between the sea and the mountains of the Holy Splendor. Yet he will come to his end—there will be no help for him. At that time Michael will arise—the great Prince, defender of your people. That will be a time of great distress, unparalleled since nations first came into existence. When that time comes, your own people will be spared—all those whose names are found written in the Book.

BOOK OF DANIEL

Then from the jaws of dragon and beast and false prophet I saw three foul spirits come; they looked like frogs and in fact were demon spirits, able to work miracles, going out to all the kings of the world to call them together for the war of the Great Day of God the Almighty . . . They called the kings together at the place called, in Hebrew, Armageddon.

BOOK OF REVELATION

Weapons will be heard in the heavens.
And in that same year the divine are enemies
They shall unjustly suppress the Holy laws
And through thunder and war shall be put to death many believers.

NOSTRADAMUS IV, 43

Poisonous clouds, made by human hands, will sink down and exterminate everything.

THE PROPHECY OF MARIA LAACH MONASTERY

Blood shall rain upon the rocks
The Sun in the east and Saturn in the west
War shall come near Orgon and near Rome a great evil
Ships will be lost and the trident taken.

NOSTRADAMUS V, 62

In my vision I saw the horses, and the riders with their breastplates of flame color, hyacinth blue and sulphur yellow; the horses had lions' heads, and fire, smoke, and sulphur were coming from their mouths. It was by these three plagues, the fire, the smoke, and the sulphur coming from their mouths, that the one third of the human race was killed.

BOOK OF REVELATION

I am going to punish the world for its wickedness
and the wicked for their guilt,
and put an end to the pride of the arrogant
and humble the haughtiness of despots.

BOOK OF ISAIAH

The crisis will come on all of a sudden and the Chastisement will be
worldwide.

MARIE-JULIE JAHENNY DE LA FAUDAIS

After terrible suffering for humankind,
Comes an even greater misery, as the cycle of the Century is renewed.
Rain, blood, famine, milk, sword and plague
In the sky shall be seen a fire, with a long tail of sparks.

NOSTRADAMUS II, 46

The nations will be in wars for four years and a great part of the
world will be destroyed. All the sects will vanish. The capital of the
world will fall. The Pope will go over the sea carrying the sign of
redemption on his forehead, and after the victory of the Pope and
the Great Monarch peace will reign on earth.

ABBOT WERDIN D'OTRANTE

PROPHECIES: 2000

For storms will rage and oceans roar
When Gabriel stands on sea and shore
And as he blows his wondrous horn
Old worlds die and new be born.

MOTHER SHIPTON

The fire shall be let loose,
A terrible death hidden within the globes
The city reduced to rubble at night by the fleet
The city on fire shall be helpful to the enemy.

NOSTRADAMUS V, 8

Cruel wars shall be scattered by the wind—whose beginnings were
by a staff; their growth and continuation by bastards—and gulled
by a revengeful hail.

MERLIN

At dawn will be seen a great fire
Noise and light reaching to the North
Within the globe are heard death and cries
Death awaits them by sword, fire, and hunger.

NOSTRADAMUS II, 91

Mars threatens us with a force of war
Seventy times shall blood be spilled
The clergy shall be reviled by those who
Refuse to learn anything from them.

NOSTRADAMUS I, 15

The armies shall battle in the sky for a long time
The tree shall fall in the middle of the city.
The holy branch cut in the face
The leader of Venice shall fall.

NOSTRADAMUS II, 11

Plagues and Epidemics

Dreadful plagues shall fall upon the race of Adam.
St. Senanus

In the hellish visions of the prophets concerning the coming years, perhaps the most fearsome are those of a coming plague the likes of which the world has not seen since the raging of the Black Death in the Middle Ages when Christendom was shaken to its foundation and death stalked everywhere—from royal palaces and castles to the humblest huts of the peasants—claiming 25 million souls. The plagues prophesied by the Old Testament, Nostradamus, and others, will slay perhaps one-third to over half of the world's population. While this may seem incredible, there are characteristics and circumstances that make the likelihood and the devastation of a pandemic increasingly likely.

The history of civilization has proven that the greatest and most determined enemies of humanity are viruses their victims never see. Today is no different, and it has been argued that we are in the midst of the most serious disease outbreak since the Middle Ages, with the tragic spread of AIDS. This late twentieth-century scourge continues to spread, despite recent breakthroughs in treatment, thanks to acute lapses in medical protocols in the Third World (through reused needles and contaminated blood) and the failure to bring the advances in care increasingly common in the First World to the poorest of nations, where the bulk of the victims are found. It is estimated that by the year 2000, over 100 million people will be infected, and there will be problems of depopulation in parts of Asia and Africa as villages and towns are wiped out.

Urban squalor and congestion are also a perfect breeding ground for a great pandemic should a devastating virus—such as Ebola—escape from its isolation in government laboratories or be introduced into the general population by an unsuspecting carrier. As international travel becomes even easier and faster, a carrier of an Ebola-like plague could board a plane in Nairobi and reach New Delhi, London, or Los Angeles before his deadly symptoms develop. In turn, his fellow passengers might become the instruments—doomed and unwitting—of wholesale death, dispersing across the globe to leave no continent untouched by the killer disease. What is worse, Ebola is only one of potentially hundreds of viruses lurking in Africa and Asia. Previously contained by geography and the impenetrable jungle, they are now being encountered by populations pushing into once-wild terrain.

Yet another fear is the mutation of an already known virus into a deadly supervirus. It is conjecture, but should AIDS somehow become airborne, the ramifications are truly horrifying, especially given the crowded conditions of cities around the globe, such as Rio, Calcutta, Tokyo, New York, Cairo, and Mexico City. Another possibility is the arrival of a new and highly drug-resistant form of tuberculosis, similar to the one already found in New York. Bubonic plague has also resurfaced in India, and Denghi Fever is now found in such cities as Atlanta and Miami.

The ultimate nightmare for virologists, of course, is that some kind of experimental virus, developed for purposes of germ warfare, escapes its imprisonment and explodes upon an unsuspecting world. Such a virus could wipe out a quarter of the Earth's human population before it is even given a name.

The rise of plagues as a facet of the end of times is a common theme in prophecies over the centuries. This is probably the result of two aspects in the lives of the individual prophets. First, many seers lived in times when it was commonly accepted that the Lord happily visits upon humanity great scourges as punishment for the incalculable sins of the world. Second, the prophets—such as Nostradamus—lived during periods when epidemics were a common occurrence and countless souls were carried off by disease.

. . . in my vision, the sanctuary, the tent of the Testimony, opened in heaven, and out came the seven angels, with the seven plagues . . .

BOOK OF REVELATION

I shall bring such distress on humanity that they will grope their way like the blind for having sinned against Yahweh. Their blood will be poured out like mud, yes, their corpses like dung; nor will their silver or gold be able to save them.

BOOK OF ZEPHIEL

With Sagittarius at its ascendant
A pond shall be stricken by the scythe
Plague, famine, death from martial hand
The Century approaches renewal.

NOSTRADAMUS I, 16

The first angel went and emptied his bowl over the earth; at once, on all the people who had been branded with the mark of the beast and had worshiped its statue, there came disgusting and virulent sores.

BOOK OF REVELATION

For as I live—declares Lord Yahweh—as sure as you have defiled my sanctuary with all your horrors and all your loathsome practices, so I too shall reject you without a glance of pity. I shall not spare you. A third of your citizens will die of plague or starve to death inside you; a third will fall by the sword round you; and a third I shall scatter to the winds . . .

BOOK OF EZEKIEL

The swords shall drip with the blood of foreign lands.
So terrible a plague shall come with the shell,
Aid will be near, but the remedy far off.

NOSTRADAMUS III, 75

The people oppressed for want of food, shall pine to death . . .
Numberless diseases shall then prevail.

ST. COLUMBKILLE

PROPHECIES: 2000

A great famine and pestilential wing
By a long rain shall come across the Arctic Pole.

NOSTRADAMUS VI, 5

These mighty tyrants will fail to do
They fail to split the world in two.
But from their acts a danger bred
An ague—leaving many dead.
And physics find no remedy
For this is worse than leprosy.

MOTHER SHIPTON

The dreadful war shall be prepared in the West
The following year shall come the plague
So horrible that young, nor old nor beast [shall survive]
Blood, fire, Mercury, Mars, Jupiter in France.

NOSTRADAMUS IX, 55

And this is the plague which Yahweh will strike all nations who
have fought against Jerusalem; their flesh will rot while they are
standing on their feet; their eyes will rot in their sockets; their
tongues will rot in their mouths.

BOOK OF ZECHARIAH

When one beholds the holy temple spoiled
The greatest of the Rhone and blessed things profaned
Through them will appear a great pestilence
The unjust King shall not condemn them.

NOSTRADAMUS VIII, 62

There will come a terrible chastisement during which many perhaps
two-thirds of the world's populations will die. This chastisement is
conditioned upon the response of humanity to the warning and the
miracle that will appear in the preceding years.

PROPHECY OF MARY AT GARABANDAL

. . . in the meantime shall be so great a plague, that two parts of
three in the world shall perish, so much so that the true owners of
fields and houses will be unknown, and there shall occur a total
decimation of the clergy . . .

NOSTRADAMUS, EPISTLE TO KING HENRY II OF FRANCE

The fifth angel emptied his bowl over the throne of the beast and its
whole empire was plunged into darkness. Men were biting their
tongues for pain, but instead of repenting for what they had done,
they cursed the God of heaven because of their pain and sores.

BOOK OF REVELATION

Plague: More than Just a Terrible Name

I t is a fact of history that more people have died from epi-demics than wars, accidents, or natural disasters. The response of the survivors of these grisly pandemics has ranged from a compassionate effort to bring comfort and dignity to the dying to absolute wild hysteria. As the 25 million poor souls were dying across Europe during the Middle Ages, some desperate and fanatical Christians, convinced that the plague was some divine retribution, formed penitential groups, called the flagellants. Dressed in sack cloth or rags, they wandered across Europe in unsightly packs, stopping at crossroads and in towns to beat themselves and bellow spiritual readings to convince the already frightened villagers that the end of the world was nigh.

Similar ideas were common during later plagues, such as that in London in 1665-1666, during which 70,000 people died. People took to wearing crude masks with scented mouth and ear holes to "purify" the air and so be spared from the disease that was ram-paging through the city. The clothes and setting may have changed from the medieval Black Death, but many were still willing to believe that the epidemic signaled the end of the world, an act of despair that implied surely no one would survive and that the Lord's retribution was upon the world. For those who think that moderns are beyond such hysteria, it might be wise to consider that there are many perfectly rational and sincere people who are convinced that AIDS, Ebola, and other deadly viruses threatening the earth are heaven sent, retribution for our countless sins to pre-pare the way for the Second Coming of what St. Malachy suppos-edly termed the "Terrible Judge who will Judge His People."

[There] shall take place a most terrible pestilence.

NOSTRADAMUS, EPISTLE TO KING HENRY II OF FRANCE

Not far from Spain, but from ancient France
Shall be elected one to lead the trembling ship.
He shall place trust in the enemy
Who shall bring a terrible plague to the realm.

NOSTRADAMUS V, 49

Seven great plagues will appear on the earth. These are a new
Metastatic Melanoma Cancer; an airborne or electromagnetically
transmitted form of AIDS; a new form of Tuberculosis; chronic
failures of the thymus and pancreas; growing vision problems; and
disorders of the Astral and Etheric Bodies, making the living
susceptible to influence from those regions beyond death, such as
"Borderland" [the boundary between the material world and the
spiritual planes].

GORDON MICHAEL SCALLION (ATTRIBUTED)

In the Cyclades, in Perinthus and Larissa
And in Sparta and the whole of the Peloponnesus
A great famine, and a great plague
Lasting nine months in the whole peninsula.

NOSTRADAMUS V, 90

The Antichrist

✠✠✠✠✠✠✠✠✠✠

The Antichrist cometh, even now there are become many Antichrists.
FIRST LETTER OF JOHN

I n the long struggle of evil to gain ascendancy in the world, no figure has been used as the preeminent example of the diabolical servant of Satan than his chief minion, perhaps even his very son, the
Antichrist. The most ardent enemy of Christ and everything the
Savior stands for, the Antichrist has been seen and heralded by many
prophets at different times, with some sensing this monster not as a
person, but a nation, a religion, a movement, or even the world itself,
corrupted by the ceaseless labors of the devil and his legions. One
thing is certain, however; when the Antichrist comes, war, pestilence,
persecution, and global despair of the spirit are sure to follow, as well
as the final climactic conflict between good and evil.

The first mention of the name Antichrist appears in the New
Testament, in the first letter of St. John (who was also the attributed
author of Revelation), but the idea of a mighty and terrible foe of
humanity emerging near the end of time is found in the long traditions of Jewish eschatology (the study of the end times, of heaven,
hell, death, and the Last Judgment). These beliefs are clear in the Old
Testament, in particular the book of Daniel, with its fiery images of a
truly fearsome tyrant who would make war upon the Chosen People.

The Antichrist assumed larger dimensions in early Christian apocalyptic writings, achieving its zenith in the Book of Revelation, with its reference to the "beast" and the "red dragon," and the assigning to the Antichrist a mysterious identifying number: 666. Using these writings, Christians since the first century have prophesied the dawning of the age of the Antichrist, using the name with remarkable frequency and attaching it to any dictator of special diabolical talent and ambition or to a deeply committed enemy of the Christian faith. Emperor Nero (who ruled from A.D. 54 to 68, until even the Romans grew so tired of him that he was overthrown), for example, was branded the Antichrist for his ruthless persecution of Christians—they were burned in arenas and thrown to wild animals—and because it suited the Christian hope of the imminent return of Christ whose second coming the Antichrist was supposed to precede.

The Antichrist was expected at the end of the first Christian millennium and during the Black Death of the fourteenth century. Martin Luther and other Protestant reformers were also called Antichrists, and in turn they called the popes—or even the institution of the papacy—the Antichrist. It was a common custom for anti-Catholics to refer to the Catholic Church in such colorful terms as the "Whore of Babylon" and to say that the number of the beast, 666, is inscribed inside the papal tiara (the triple crown worn by the popes until the modern era).

Michel de Nostradamus did much to reintroduce the notion of the Antichrist into popular culture, removing the tyrant from a strictly religious and eschatological environment to one of a worldly power who posed a threat to all. Nostradamus was also responsible for two other innovations concerning the Antichrist.

First, his prophecies pointed to three Antichrists to come.

Increasingly horrendous, the Antichrists have been identified as Napoleon, Hitler, and an as yet unidentified third beast to appear within the next few years. It is thought that Nostradamus actually gave the date for this Antichrist—cryptically given the name Mabus—to be in ascendancy: July 1999. If the coming years prove the rise of the Antichrist, the world can only hope that he is not as terrifying and destructive as Nostradamus and others have foreseen.

❈

Besmirched by murder and enormous adulteries
A great enemy of all humanity
He shall be more terrible than his ancestors, uncles, and fathers
In steel, fire, and water, bloody and inhuman.

NOSTRADAMUS X, 10

❈

But the coming of the wicked One will be marked by Satan being at work in all kinds of counterfeit miracles and signs and wonders, and every wicked deception aimed at those who are on the way to destruction because they would not accept the love of the truth and so be saved.

2 THESSALONIANS

❈

One who revives the infernal gods of Hannibal
The terror of mankind,
There never was more horror, nor will be spoken of more evil days.

NOSTRADAMUS II, 30

❈

By the time that the Antichrist is twenty years old, the world will have lost its faith.

BERNARD DE BUSTO

※

THE BEAST OF APOCALYPSE: 666

Then I saw a second beast; it emerged from the ground; it had two horns like a lamb, but made a noise like a dragon. This second beast was servant to the first beast, and extended its authority everywhere, making the world and all its people worship the first beast, which had had the fatal wound and had been healed. And it worked great miracles, even to calling down fire from heaven onto the earth while people watched.

Through the miracles which it was allowed to do on behalf of the first beast, it was able to win over the people of the world and persuade them to put up a statue in honor of the beast that had been wounded by the sword and still lived . . . anyone who refused to worship the statue of the beast [was] put to death. He compelled everyone—small and great alike, rich and poor, slave and citizen—to be branded on the right hand or on the forehead, and made it illegal for anyone to buy or sell anything unless he had been branded with the name of the beast or with the number of its name . . . the number of the beast: it is the number of a man; the number 666.

BOOK OF REVELATION

※

※

The fourth beast
is to be a fourth kingdom on earth,
different from all other kingdoms.
It will devour the whole world
trample it underfoot and crush it.

BOOK OF DANIEL

❖

... a king will arise, a proud-faced ingenious-minded man. His
power will grow greater and greater, though not through any power
of his own; he will plot incredible schemes, he will succeed in
whatever he undertakes, he will destroy powerful men and the holy
ones, God's people. Such will be his resourcefulness of mind that all
his treacherous activities will succeed. He will grow arrogant of heart
and destroy many people by taking them unawares. He will
challenge the power of the prince of princes but, without any human
intervention, he will be broken.

BOOK OF DANIEL

❖

[There] shall arise another king, a crafty man, who shall hold rule
for a short pace; in those days there shall be all manner of evil, even
the death of the race of men from the east even unto Babylon. And
thereafter death and famine and sword in the land of Canaan even
unto Rome.

APOCALYPSE OF THOMAS

❖

❖

The Antichrist soon will annihilate the three
His war shall endure for seven and twenty years
The heretics are dead, imprisoned, exiled
Blood, bodies, water, and scarlet hail covering the earth.

NOSTRADAMUS VIII, 77

In 1999 and seven months
From the sky shall come the grand King of Terror
He shall resurrect the great King of the Mongols
Before and after, Mars shall reign happily.

NOSTRADAMUS X, 72

It cannot happen until the Great Revolt has taken place and there
has appeared the wicked One, the Lost One, the Enemy, who raises
himself above every so-called God or object of worship to enthrone
himself in God's sanctuary and flaunts the claim that he is God.

2 THESSALONIANS

This man will be known by a barbaric name
So that three sisters shall receive from destiny
He shall speak in word and deed to a great people
And shall have renown greater than any other.

NOSTRADAMUS I, 76

Following the birth of the Antichrist, most of humanity will be as corrupt as the world—the sheep will be transformed into the godless or fall into heresy. Churches will be empty and in ruins, priests will have little zeal for souls and pious souls will be few. Most people will be given up to all imaginable vices.

POPE GREGORY I THE GREAT

The great Monarch and the great Pope will precede Antichrist. The nations will be at war for four years and a great part of the world will be destroyed. The Pope will go over the sea carrying the sign of Redemption on his forehead. The great Monarch will come to restore peace and the Pope will share in the victory.

ABBOT WERDIN D'OTRANTE

After the birth of the Antichrist, most people will possess something that they stole and they will be greedy, godless, selfish, and hard-hearted. Justice will disappear from the earth so that humanity will know not law, order, and nor discipline. The world will be filled with murderers and robbers. Priests will act like wolves, care nothing for spiritual things, and live with women . . . righteousness will so decrease, and impiety, avarice, desire, and lust will so greatly increase, that if there shall then happen to be any good men, they will be prey to the wicked.

LACTANTIUS

CANDIDATES FOR THE ANTICHRIST

The third (and one barely needs to add the most horrid) of Nostradamus's Antichrists is perhaps alive and working in the world today preparing the way for his rise to global domination. His coming has long been anticipated by Christians, and several prophets have even tried to fix the date of his birth. In 1890, the seer Gabriel Jogard put the birthday of Christ's great foe at 1962. Seemingly confirming this, the American prophet Jeane Dixon (who claims among other things to have foretold the assassination of President John F. Kennedy) had a vision that the Antichrist was born on February 5, 1962.

More clues as to his possible identification are found in legend, traditions, and the prophecies of Nostradamus. According to Jewish legend, the fiendish son of Satan is named Armilus and carries the distinguishing marks of having one eye bigger than the other, being partially deaf, and possibly walking with a limp. Nostradamus uses such names as *Mabus* and *Alus* (most likely anagrams, as the King of Prophets kept things deliberately obscure) for him and states that his rise will be heralded by an eclipse of the sun. The eclipse will be darker than any ever seen, save for that which caused the earth to tremble after the Crucifixion of Christ. The next such solar eclipse will come on August 11, 1999, a date perfectly in keeping with Nostradamus's infamous quatrain about the King of Terror. Biblical tradition also associates the Antichrist with the mysterious number of the Beast: 666. Meanwhile, Coptic Egyptian specialists in the End Times are quite adamant that the Antichrist is laboring even now, in the Middle East, to bring war and destruction on a global scale to pave the way for his material and spiritual conquest of humanity. We are told to await his emergence in the Middle East and then his arrival in triumph in New York within the next years. From there, his diabolical career will proceed swiftly, culminating in the Third World War and his claim to the throne of the Earth.

After the birth of the Antichrist, the world will be faithless and degenerate.

ST. JOHN CHRYSOSTOM

The great Vicar shall be restored to his proper place, but he shall return—forsaken—to the sanctuary destroyed by the pagans, when the Old and New Testament are taken and burned. After that, the Antichrist shall be the infernal prince. And in this last time, all the Christian realms and those of the unbelievers shall live in fear for the space of years, and there shall be terrible wars and battles. Towns, cities, and buildings will be burned, ruined, and destroyed . . . so many evils shall be committed by the infernal prince, Satan, that virtually the entire world shall be broken and laid waste.

NOSTRADAMUS, EPISTLE TO KING HENRY II OF FRANCE

[A] king shall arise out of Syria, born from an evil spirit, the overthrower and destroyer of the human race.

LACTANTIUS

Mabus shall die soon, and
Upon people and beasts shall come a horrible destruction
Vengeance will suddenly be seen
Blood, hand, thirst, famine when the comet passes.

NOSTRADAMUS II, 62

The mystery of wickedness is already at work, but let him who is restraining it once be removed and the wicked One shall appear openly. The Lord will destroy him with the breath of his mouth and will annihilate him with his glorious appearance at his coming.

2 THESSALONIANS

... four great beasts are four kings who will rise up from the earth ...

BOOK OF DANIEL

Economic Ruin

Financial disaster and destruction of poverty will cause many tears to fall.
PROPHECY OF WARSAW

October 29, 1929. In one of the darkest days in American history, the stock market crashed, the final avalanche in the economic storm that had been gathering in the previous weeks. Buyers of stocks, desperate to sell, took greater and greater losses in a final attempt to salvage a fraction of their money. Within weeks, banks and savings and loans were bankrupt, businesses were failing, and more and more workers were unemployed and out in the street. The Great Depression swept across the globe, bringing economic hardships to virtually every country. Within four years, fascists had risen to power in Italy, Germany, and Japan. Within ten years, the world was at war.

Catching the world completely by surprise, the Great Depression was definite proof that economic catastrophe can be just as devastating as a comet striking from heaven or a massive earthquake. Among the many possible fates awaiting humanity, perhaps the most likely of them is economic catastrophe. As the stock market crashes of 1987 and 1997 and the recessions of the late 1970s and 1990–1992 proved, economic downturns and financial crises are a reality of life, with real-world consequences for virtually all segments of society. What is more, unlike an earthquake or a hurricane, a depression—or the deflationary recession expected by some economists—will have no geographic limits, leaving no one safe from its effects and no place to escape it.

Nostradamus, Mother Shipton, and others of past centuries did not live in a time filled with transnational corporations, international monetary policy, or global mutual funds. Nevertheless, they did see economic crises, describing them in often apocalyptic terms or within the context of human failings. Perhaps the most accurate prophecy comes from Abraham Lincoln in a letter written in 1864, which speaks with amazing accuracy of conditions in late twentieth-century America.

❖

I see in the near future a crisis approaching that unnerves me and causes me to tremble for the safety of my country. As a result of the war, corporations have been enthroned, and an era of corruption in high places will follow, and the money power of the country will endeavor to prolong its reign by working upon the prejudices of the people until all wealth is aggregated in a few hands and the Republic is destroyed. I feel at this moment more anxiety for the safety of my country than ever before, even in the midst of war.

ABRAHAM LINCOLN
(NOVEMBER 21, 1864, LETTER TO
COL. WILLIAM F. ELKINS)

❖

. . . at the end of this century America will be destroyed economically by a series of natural disasters.

THERESE NEUMANN

❖

❖

God will punish the world when men have devised marvelous
inventions that will lead them to forgetting God. They will have
horseless carriages, and they will fly like birds.

BLESSED REMBORDT

❇

The call of the unwanted bird having been heard
Upon the chimney
Bushels of wheat shall rise so high
That men shall devour their fellow men.

NOSTRADAMUS II, 75

❇

No more will treacherous gold and silver be
Nor earthly wealth, nor toilsome servitude,
But one fast friendship and one mode of life
Will be with the glad people, and all things
Will common be, and equal light of life.

SIBYLLINE ORACLES

❇

Mourn, mourn for this great city
whose lavish living has made a fortune
for every owner of a sea-going ship;
Ruined within a single hour.

BOOK OF REVELATION

❇

❇

Owing to the massive physical changes that are coming to the United States through earthquakes and volcanic eruptions, the nation's economy and the government will collapse. In the rebuilding of the United States, there will be reborn the original thirteen colonies.

GORDON MICHAEL SCALLION (ATTRIBUTED)

❊

Before the war breaks out again, food will be scarce and expensive. There will be little work for the workers, and fathers will hear their children crying for food.

THE ECSTATIC OF TOURS

❊

The copies swollen with gold and silver
Which were thrown into the lake and fire after the theft
Being found after the fire is extinguished.
All scrips and bonds shall be expunged.

NOSTRADAMUS VIII, 28

❊

Famine will spread over the nations, and nation will rise against nation, kingdom against kingdom, and states against states in our own country and in foreign lands; and they will destroy each other, caring not for the blood and lives of their neighbors, of their families, or of their own lives.

BRIGHAM YOUNG

❊

❊

On the day of Yahweh's sacrifice, I shall punish the courtiers, the royal princes and all who dress in outlandish clothes. On that day I shall punish all who go up the Step and fill the Temple of their lords, with violence and deceit.

BOOK OF ZEPHANIAH

There'll be a sign for all to see
Be sure that it will certain be.
Then love shall die and marriage cease
And nations wane as babes decrease.

MOTHER SHIPTON

The kings shall false promise make and talk just for talking's sake and nations plan horrific war. The like as never seen before and taxes rise and lively down and nations wear perpetual frown.

BOOK OF ZEPHANIAH

THE PAPACY

A remarkable Pope will be seated upon the papal throne,
under the special protection of the angels.
JOACHIM DA FIORE

The time approaches when princes and people will renounce the
authority of the Pope.
ST. HILDEGARD OF BINGEN

In the 2000-year history of the popes—stretching from St. Peter to John Paul II—the leaders of the Catholic Church have been arrested, tortured, imprisoned, poisoned, beheaded, strangled, and exiled by kings, emperors, and tyrants. Their enemies have ranged from Justinian and Emperor Frederick Barbarossa to Napoleon Bonaparte, Josef Stalin, and Adolf Hitler, and the imminent extinction of the Holy See has been predicted in nearly every century. And still the papacy endures as a testament to the faith of the Catholic Church and the consummate skill of the popes themselves in overcoming the most seemingly insurmountable foes and obstacles.

The prophecies concerning the papacy would seem to mirror the historical life of the Holy See. Dark days are looming ahead, but the popes will survive to be restored to their rightful place as leaders of the Catholic Church. Still, the days ahead will be difficult, especially if the prophecies of the Church's own saints are proven correct. Nostradamus, too, devotes much of his prophetic effort (as seen in his quatrains) to the popes, although his often peculiar and obscure imagery is especially so when writing about the popes. This was necessary because of the constant threat from arrest by religious authorities in sixteenth-century France, particularly for making prophecies about the popes. The visions of Nostradamus reveal blood, scandal, death, and intrigue.

Readers will probably be surprised at the number of prophecies relating to the popes. This is largely the result of the historical significance of the Church's leaders, most so during the eras when many of the most notable prophecies were made, namely the Middle Ages and the sixteenth century. The popes represented not only the hierarchy of the Church, but were considered the embodiment of the entire Catholic faith. Thus, the prophecies relating to the popes assumed a meaning relative both to the papacy itself and the faith they headed.

The volume of the prophecies poses a number of problems as the millennium approaches. It scarcely seems possible that the majority of the events forecast could take place within the next few years. If even a few of the prophecies should be correct, however, it would seem that the new century marks a time of immense tribulation for the Church. The events described would also point to the time after the reign of Pope John Paul II, despite the pontiff's personal aspirations of surviving at least to the year 2000 to celebrate the jubilee of the Church's history.

Two themes that occur in the prophecies are the war made upon the pontiffs by the Great Enemy—the Antichrist—and the coming of the Angelic Pastor. The popes will apparently be driven from Rome (indeed, Pope St. Pius X beheld a ghastly vision of this) and the faithful will be forced to watch the Church go for a time without a

Supreme Pastor in Rome. It is even possible that the Antichrist—or at least the enemies of the Catholic faith—may replace the pope with an antipope, or the Church may face a schism with the depressing prospect of rival papal claimants struggling for the papal throne for some years.

The solution to these disasters will be brought by the Angelic Pastor, a saintly pontiff blessed and protected by the angels. According to Nostradamus, this pontiff will come from the 48th degree latitude (a line running through the sees of Munich, Vienna, and Orléans) and will guide the Church by his faith and much of the world by his boundless optimism and grace in the trials coming during the reign of the Antichrist.

By the appearance of false holiness
The seat shall be delivered to the enemy
In the night when it was thought all was safe
Those of Liege will march near Brabant.

NOSTRADAMUS VI, 30

Through the power of three temporal kings
Shall the Holy See be taken to another place
Where the substance of the body and spirit
Shall be restored and accepted as the true seat.

NOSTRADAMUS VIII, 99

A man of remarkable sanctity will be [a] successor to the Pontifical
chair. Through him God will work so many prodigies that all men
shall revere him, and no person will dare to oppose his precepts . . .
He will preach the gospel in person.

JOACHIM DA FIORE

Roman Pontiff, beware of nearing the city
Watered by two rivers
There shall you spit up blood
You and yours when the roses bloom.

NOSTRADAMUS II, 97

Famine, pestilence, war and fraud will lay waste to the Italian
Kingdom . . . The Supreme pastor will hold the keys of Heaven but
will be deprived of his earthly kingdom.

VENERABLE MAGDALENE PORZAT

. . . there will be a great Pope, who will be most eminent in sanctity
and most perfect in every quality. This Pope shall have with him the
Great Monarch, a most virtuous man, who shall be a scion of the
holy race of the French kings. This Great Monarch shall assist the
Pope in the reformation of the whole earth.

CAESARIUS OF ARLES

We have to be prepared to suffer, before long, great trials which will require of us the disposition to sacrifice even our life . . . for Christ. Through your prayers and mine, it is still possible to diminish this trial, but it is no longer possible to avert it, because only in this manner can the Church be effectively renewed. How many times has the renewal of the Church been brought about in blood! It will not be different this time.

POPE JOHN PAUL II

The great pope shall be captured while sailing
The clergy are thrown into uproar
A second, absent, elected, loses his power.

NOSTRADAMUS V, 15

The mighty star shall shine for seven days
And a cloud will cause the sun to appear double,
The great mastiff shall howl through the night
When the mighty Pontiff changes his country.

NOSTRADAMUS II, 41

. . . the Catholic clergy and faithful of the true and lawful Pope will be elected, who will be a man of deep holiness and goodness; he will come from the surviving monastic orders.

CAPUCHIN FRIAR

The blood of the men of the Church
Will be poured forth in such abundance as water
And for a long time it will not be stemmed
Alas, Alas! Ruin and grief for the clergy.

NOSTRADAMUS VIII, 98

For four years will the seat be kept well.
Then shall come one of libidinous lifestyle
Ravenna and Pisa, Verona will aid him
Desirous of raising up the papal cross.

NOSTRADAMUS VI, 26

On the sea shall the red one be captured by pirates
Because of him the peace shall be threatened
Through a false deed he shall reveal ire and greed
The army of the mighty pontiff doubled.

NOSTRADAMUS, V, 44

The pope will change his residence and the Church will not be
defended for twenty-five months or more because, during all that
time there will be no Pope in Rome ... After many tribulations, a
Pope shall be elected out of those who survived the persecutions.

JOÃO DE VATIGUERRO

When the tomb of the great Roman shall be found
A pope shall be elected the next day
He will not be approved by the Senate
His blood poisoned in the sacred chalice.

NOSTRADAMUS III, 65

He who shall be adorned with the great cloak
Shall be compelled to commit some act
The twelve red ones shall soil the cover
Under murder, murder shall be committed.

NOSTRADAMUS IV, 11

A new pastor of the Church will come from the shore of Dalmatia through a celestial miracle, and in simplicity of heart decorated with the doctrines of Jesus Christ. Peace will be brought back to the world.

RUDOLPH GEKNER

After the See has been held for seventeen years
Five will change in the same space of time
Then one will be elected
Who will not be too acceptable to the Romans.

NOSTRADAMUS V, 92

Violent hands will be laid on the Supreme head of the Catholic
Church; bishops and priests will be persecuted, and schisms will be
provoked, and confusion reign amid all classes. Times will come, so
pre-eminently bad, that it will seem as if the enemies of Christ and
of His Holy Church, which He founded with His blood, were
about to triumph over her. But the priesthood will remain firm and
resolute, and good people will adhere to that body.

BISHOP GEORGE MICHAEL WITTMANN

The time approaches when princes and people will renounce the
authority of the Pope. Individual countries will prefer their own
Church leaders to the Pope . . . Church property will be secularized.
Priests will be persecuted. After the birth of the Antichrist, heretics
shall preach their false faith undisturbed, and Christians shall have
grave doubts about the holy faith.

ST. HILDEGARD OF BINGEN

Toward the end of the world the tyrants and the hostile people will
suddenly rob the prelates and clergy of the Church of all their
possessions and grievously afflict and martyr them. The ones who
heap the most abuse upon them will be held in greatest esteem . . .
At that time, the Pope and the Cardinals will have to flee Rome
under difficult circumstances to a place where he will be unknown.
The Pope will die a cruel death in exile; the sufferings of the Church
will be greater than at any time in her history.

BROTHER JOHN OF THE CLEFT ROCK

A remarkable Pope will be seated upon the papal throne, under the special protection of the angels. Holy and gentle, he will correct all the wrongs, recover the states of the Church, and reunite the exiled temporal rulers ... He shall reunite the Eastern to the Western Churches, and thus only faith will be in vigor.

JOACHIM DA FIORE

With Mars adverse shall the monarchy
Of the great fisherman be brought to ruin
A young, black red shall take over the hierarchy
The traitors will act on a day of fog.

NOSTRADAMUS VI, 25

The false message, about a rigged election
Shall spread throughout the city.
Voices shall be purchased and the chapel stained with blood.
Another contests the rule.

NOSTRADAMUS VIII, 20

Then from that branch that has for so long been barren—coming from the 50th degree of latitude—one will come who shall reform the whole of the Christian Church.

NOSTRADAMUS, EPISTLE TO KING HENRY II OF FRANCE

PROPHECİES: 2000

Among the red hats will be new quarrels and schisms
When the Sabine [one from near Rome] will be elected
Terrible sophisms shall be produced against him.
And Rome shall be injured by those of Albanois.

NOSTRADAMUS V, 46

※

Not far from Spain, but from ancient France
Shall be elected one to lead the trembling ship.
He shall place trust in the enemy
Who shall bring a terrible plague to the realm.

NOSTRADAMUS V, 49

※

The clergy will be persecuted, priests will be massacred, churches
will be closed; but only for a short time. The Holy Father will be
forced to flee Rome.

BLESSED ANNA MARIA TAIGI

※

O mighty Rome, thy ruin approaches
Not of thy walls, but of thy blood
The cruel one by letters shall make so horrible a notch
Sharp steel thrust all the way to the sleeve.

NOSTRADAMUS X, 65

※

※

The Pope will change his residence; the Church will not be defended for the duration of twenty-five months, and more, because during all this time there will be no Pope, no Emperor of Rome and no ruler of France.

JOÃO DE VATIGUERRO

✦

In the world shall be made a ruler
Who shall not have peace nor a long life
Then the Fishing Boat (the Barque of Peter)
Shall be lost, governed to its great detriment.

NOSTRADAMUS I, 4

✦

There will be two more popes after Pope Paul VI. One of the popes will have a very short reign. After that will come the end times, though they will not bring the end of the world.

PROPHECY OF MARY AT GARABANDAL

✦

By the passing of the very old pontiff
Shall be chosen a Roman of good age
It shall be said that he weakens the Seat
And shall live long and be of fierce courage.

NOSTRADAMUS V, 56

✦

✦

Some day, the Pope will flee from Rome, accompanied only by four cardinals.

HELEN WALLRAFF

Malachy's Last Popes

Aside from the often grim prophecies by Nostradamus concerning the future of the papacy, the most famous prophetic work on the Holy See is that supposedly written by St. Malachy (d. 1148), the archbishop of Armagh and a famous leader of the Church in Ireland. Malachy's prophecies are a listing of the popes from Pope Celestine II (r. 1143-1144) to the last pope, Peter II. The popes are cataloged not by name but through concise, descriptive, and frequently enigmatic mottoes.

Question has long been made as to the authenticity of the prophecies, and it has been theorized—first by a Jesuit historian in the seventeenth century—that they are a complete forgery. Whether true or not, Malachy's prophecies nevertheless make for intriguing reading. According to one estimate, there are only two popes left after Pope John Paul II (whose motto is *De Labore Solis*, "Of the Labor of the Sun"). The next pontiff is called by Malachy the *Gloria Olivae* ("The Glory of the Olive"), possibly an allusion to the efforts of John Paul II's successor to promote peace in a war-torn world. It is possible that this pontiff will fail as after him will supposedly come the last pontiff. Peter II, called *Petrus Romanus* ("Peter the Roman"), will ascend to the papacy in what is obviously a frightening era. Malachy writes:

In the final persecution of the Roman Church
There will reign Peter the Roman
Who will feed his flock among many trials
Then the seven-hilled city will be destroyed
And the dreadful Judge will judge his people.

Religion

Then shall there come a fiercer persecution of the Church than ever.
NOSTRADAMUS, EPISTLE TO KING HENRY II OF FRANCE

I f it is true that persecutions make a religion stronger, then the next few years—as seen by the prophets—will leave the world's faiths very strong indeed, although it is possible there will be very few believers left alive to give worship. The next years will possibly bring a massive persecution of traditional religion, through the machinations of the Antichrist, and a severe loss of life among the clergy and religious through plagues, social strife, natural disaster, and war.

According to a number of prophets, the clergy will only add to their suffering by their failure to uphold their oaths of obedience and chastity, their hypocrisy, and their obsession with purely material matters. St. Columbkille of Ireland, for example, speaks of the clergy being led into error, while St. Antony of the Desert foresaw the surrendering of humanity to the spirit of the age. Still others, including Cheiro, see the Churches torn from within by heresy and schism.

The effect of these enormous trials will be twofold, depending upon the prophets one chooses to believe. Nostradamus and the Christian prophets see the torment as a purgative, cleansing the faith and leaving those who remain true to their belief stronger and refined in the spirit. The faiths themselves will be equally purified, although some seers predict that the tribulations will be part of the Rapture, the apocalyptic time preceding the Second Coming when the holy on the earth are taken away (perhaps physically lifted into the heavens) leaving the rest of the general—and embarrassingly sinful—population to fend for themselves. Intertwined with this view is the idea that the cessation of the suffering will be announced by none other than the return of Christ to pass a final judgment upon the human race.

A rather different sense of the purpose of the suffering is explored by more modern visionaries, such as Cheiro, Madame Helena Blavatsky, and Gordon Michael Scallion. Their prophecies indicate that the time of suffering is part of a transformation of the world away from traditional religion toward a global, new age, spiritual unity. Cheiro writes that "perfection cannot be attained until all religions have become merged into one." It is thought that once all faiths are one—having presumably resolved the countless doctrinal and spiritual differences that exist—the long struggles caused by religion will be resolved and an age of peace will descend miraculously.

❊

Priests and servants of the Church will be reduced to misery, the youth led by atheism, and republics will be established in the whole world. And all will be destroyed by wars.

PASTOR BARTHOLOMAEUS

❊

. . . the Church will have revolution within itself. Strange creeds will be preached from all pulpits.

COUNT LOUIS HAMON (CHEIRO)

❊

❊

The Church of God shall be persecuted
And the sacred temples will be pillaged
The child shall cast out his mother nude in her shirt
The Arabs shall be allies of the Poles.

NOSTRADAMUS V, 73

A world-wide Warning will be experienced by everyone on earth. It will be a call to humanity to repent and return to God. A great miracle will then occur in the late winter or early spring within one year after the warning, and a permanent "sign" will remain for all time at Garabandal and other chosen places where Mary has appeared.

PROPHECY OF MARY AT GARABANDAL

In those days evils shall abound: there shall be no respectors of persons, hymns shall cease out of the House of the Lord, truth shall be no more, covetousness shall abound among the priests; an upright man shall not be found.

APOCALYPSE OF THOMAS

In the final days, false prophets and corrupters shall come in swarms, and the sheep shall be changed into wolves, and love into hatred . . .

DIDACHE

... changes are coming, this may be sure—an evolution or revolution in the ideas of religious thought. The BASIS of it for the world will eventually come out of Russia; not Communism, no! But rather that which is the basis of the same, as the Christ taught—His kind of communism!

EDGAR CAYCE

The blood of the men of the Church
Shall be poured forth in such abundance as water
And for a long time it will not be stemmed
Alas, alas! Ruin and grief for the clergy.

NOSTRADAMUS VIII, 98

The fifth period of the Church, which began circa 1520, will end with the arrival of the holy Pope and of the powerful Monarch who is called "Help From God" because he will restore everything. The fifth period is one of affliction, desolation, humiliation and poverty for the Church. Jesus Christ will purify His people through cruel wars, famines, plagues, epidemics and other horrible calamities. He will also afflict and weaken the Latin Church with many heresies. It is a period of defections, calamities and exterminations. Those Christians who survive the sword, plague and famines, will be few on earth.

VENERABLE BARTHOLOMEW HOLZHAUSER

The Warning, like the Chastisement, is a fearful thing for the good as well as the wicked. It will draw the good closer to God and warn the wicked that the end of times are coming.

PROPHECY OF MARY AT GARABANDAL

Churches shall be built up again as before, the clergy shall be reinstated to their former place, until they fall back once more into prostitution and luxury and perpetrate a thousand crimes.

NOSTRADAMUS, EPISTLE TO KING HENRY II OF FRANCE

Then I saw some thrones, and I saw *those who are given the power to be judges take* their seats on them. I saw the souls of all who had been beheaded for having witnessed for Jesus and for having preached God's word, and those who refused to worship the beast or his statue and would not accept the brand mark on their foreheads or hands; they came to life, and reigned with Christ . . .

BOOK OF REVELATION

In a short time shall sacrifices be resumed
Those who oppose shall be martyred
There shall be no monks, abbots, nor novices
Honey shall be more expensive than wax.

NOSTRADAMUS I, 44

The end of the world will come when faith in godliness shall perish from men, and justice is hidden away in the world, and men become renegades and, living on unholy enterprises, commit deeds of shame, and acts, dastardly and evil; and no man takes account of the godly, but even in their senselessness, fond fools, they destroy themselves, rejoicing in acts of violence, turning their hands to deeds of bloodshed.

SIBYLLINE ORACLES

For a time Religion will save herself from catastrophe by abolishing her Bishops' "palaces," her gilded ceremonies and her alliances with Monarchs.

COUNT LOUIS HAMON (CHEIRO)

In the sacred temples shall be committed scandals
That shall be misconstrued for honors and praises.
By one whose medals are carved on silver and gold.
The end will be in strange torments.

NOSTRADAMUS VI, 9

In the last days shall false Christs come and stir expectations, saying, I am the Christ, now come into the world.

APOCALYPSE OF PETER

PROPHECIES: 2000

Darkness will be preferred to light, and death will be thought more profitable than life; no one will raise his eyes to heaven; the pious will be deemed insane, the impious wise; the madman will be thought a brave man, and the wicked will be esteemed as good.

HERMES TRISMEGISTUS

In the last times there shall be many dissensions among the peoples, blasphemy, iniquity, envy, and villainy, indolence, pride and intemperance, so that every man shall speak that which pleaseth him. And my priests shall not have peace among themselves, but shall sacrifice unto me with deceitful minds: therefore I will not look upon them.

APOCALYPSE OF THOMAS

The empty synagogues, without fruit
Shall be received by the infidels
In Babylon, the daughter of the persecuted
Miserable and sad, they shall cut her wings.

NOSTRADAMUS VIII, 96

. . . you will be handed over to be tortured and put to death; and you will be hated by all nations on account of my name.

GOSPEL OF MATTHEW

The deceiver shall be put into the ditch
And be bound for a time
The cleric joins the leader with his cross
Leaning to the right shall draw the contented.

NOSTRADAMUS VIII, 95

Of the three sects—Lutheran, Catholic, and Muslim—that which is the middlemost, by the deeds of its followers shall be brought into ruin. Lutheranism—utterly in Europe and the most part in Africa—shall be replaced by Islam, by means of the poor in spirit . . .

NOSTRADAMUS, EPISTLE TO KING HENRY II OF FRANCE

Under the guise of humanity, Religion will creep back to her cradle of poverty and persecution, and in the next hundred years there will be as many religious sects in the World as there are pieces of supposed "true Cross" in existence at the present time.

COUNT LOUIS HAMON (CHEIRO)

At the founding of a new sect
The bones of the great Roman pontiff will be found
The tomb covered in marble will appear
In April will the earth quake, badly buried.

NOSTRADAMUS VI, 66

Followers of Sects, much trouble for the accuser
A beast in the theater prepares the stage and plot
The author shall be famous by deeds of ancient times
By sects shall the world be confused and schismatic.

NOSTRADAMUS I, 45

Falsehood will characterize that class of men who will sit in judgment to pass sentence according to law: between the father and his son, litigations will subsist. The clergy of the holy church will be addicted to pride and injustice. Women will abandon feelings of delicacy, and cohabit with men out of wedlock.

ST. SENANUS

. . . perfection cannot be attained until all religions have become merged into one. This, the apparently "impossible," is every day becoming more and more probable. The sway and power of State-supported creeds is on the decline, or splitting into so many sects that they are "like sheep without a shepherd."

COUNT LOUIS HAMON (CHEIRO)

Mankind will be purified through immense suffering . . . especially the clergy, who will be robbed of all property.

ST. HILDEGARD OF BINGEN

The era of the Antichrist will be near when the measure of injustice will overflow and when wickedness has grown to immense proportions, when Christians adore heresy, and the unjust trample upon the servants of God.

RICHARD ROLLE OF HAMPOLE

The most Holy Trinity confirmed the desire of my Queen, assuring that God will bless all those who, by their support and help, contribute in the making of the Holy Statue, as well as all those who help spread this devotion (to Our Lady of Good Success) throughout the centuries, making known its origin and these apparitions in the 20th century. This will be a time of great corruption of customs . . . the sacred sacrament of Holy Orders will be ridiculed, oppressed and despised, for in doing this, one scorns and defiles the Church of God, and even God Himself, represented by His priests. The Demon will try to persecute the Ministers of the Lord in every possible way. . . .

SR. MARIANNE DE JESUS TORRES

. . . many will fall away; people will betray one another and hate one another. Many false prophets will arise; they will deceive many, and with the increase of lawlessness, love in most people will grow cold; but anyone who stands firm to the end will be saved.

GOSPEL OF MATTHEW

But when all this has befallen, then God the Creator of all things
will look on that which has come to pass, and will stop the disorder
by the counterforce of his will, which is the good. He will call back
to the right path those who have gone astray; he will cleanse the
world of evil, washing it away with floods, burning it out with the
fiercest fire, and expelling it with war and pestilence.

HERMES TRISMEGISTUS

The clergy of the holy church will be addicted to pride and injustice;
the advantages they will aim at shall be the possession of worldly
substance.

ST. SENANUS

Alas, how tormented shall be a great people
And the Holy Laws in utter ruins
Christianity is troubled by other laws
When new sources of gold and silver are found.

NOSTRADAMUS I, 53

Great carnage shall be made, justice shall be outraged, multitudinous
evils, great suffering shall prevail . . . They will plunder the property
of the church.

ST. COLUMBKILLE

In the days of peace that are to come after the desolation of revolutions and wars, before the end of the world, the Christians will become so lax in their religion that they will refuse to receive the Sacrament of Confirmation, saying "it is an unnecessary Sacrament."

ST. VINCENT FERRER

During this period, many men will abuse the freedom of conscience conceded to them. It is of such men that Jude the Apostle spoke when he said: "These men blaspheme whatever they do not understand; and they corrupt whatever they know naturally as irrational animals do . . . They will ridicule Christian simplicity; they will call it folly and nonsense, but they will have the highest regard for advanced knowledge, and for the skill by which the axioms of law, the precepts of morality, the Holy Canons and religious dogmas are clouded by senseless questions and elaborate arguments."

VENERABLE BARTHOLOMEW HOLZHAUSER

It was revealed to me that through the intercession of the Mother of God, all heresies will disappear. This victory over heresies has been reserved by Christ for His Blessed Mother . . . Before the Second Coming of Christ, Mary must, more than ever, shine in mercy, might and grace in order to bring unbelievers into the Catholic Faith.

VENERABLE MARIA DE AGREDA

He who shall be charged with the destruction of
Churches and sects, changed by fantasy
He shall damage the rocks rather than the living
By filling ears with ornate speeches.

NOSTRADAMUS I, 96

For in those days there will be great distress, unparalleled since God
created the world, and such as will never be again. And if the Lord
had not shortened that time, no human being would have survived;
but he did shorten the time, for the sake of the elect whom he chose.
And if anyone says to you then, "Look, here is the Christ" or,
"Look, he is there," do not believe it; from false Christs and false
prophets will arise and produce signs and portents to deceive the
elect, if that were possible.

GOSPEL OF MARK

Then Jesus began to tell them, "Take care that no one deceives
you. Many will come using my name and saying, 'I am he,' and
they will deceive many. When you hear of wars and rumors of
wars, do not be alarmed; this is something that must happen, but
the end will not be yet. For nation will fight against nation, and
kingdom against kingdom. There will be earthquakes in various
places; there will be famines. This is the beginning of the birth-
pangs."

GOSPEL OF MARK

The monks will have to leave their monasteries, and the nuns will be driven from their convents, especially in Italy . . .

ABBESS MARIA STEINER

❊

. . . Forgive one another. Love one another. Serve one another. Pray for the Church. Pray for priests. Return to the Sacraments, dear little children. Confess your sins while the sun shines. Sacrifice yourselves for the conversion of sinners and for peace in the world. All of you are children of God. All are loved.

PROPHECY OF MARY AT BETANIA

❊

Temples blessed in the early Roman fashion
Shall reject the weakened foundations
Adhering to their early human laws
Expelling nearly all of the worship of saints.

NOSTRADAMUS II, 8

❊

They will no longer love this world around us, this incomparable work of God, this glorious structure which he has built, this sum of good made up of many diverse forms, this instrument whereby the will of God operates in that which he has made, ungrudgingly favoring man's welfare.

HERMES TRISMEGISTUS

❊

❊

Many Cardinals, many Bishops, and many Priests are on the path of perdition and they take many souls with them. To the Eucharist, there is given less and less importance. We should avoid the wrath of God on us by our good efforts. If you ask pardon with your sincere soul God will pardon you. It is I, your mother, who through the intercession of St. Michael, wish to say that you amend, that you are already in the last warnings and that I love you much and do not want your condemnation. Ask us sincerely and we will give to you. You should sacrifice more. Think of the passion of Jesus.

PROPHECY OF MARY AT GARABANDAL

❉

[A] horrid king shall be praised by his followers for shedding more blood of clerics than has been done of wine. The king shall commit unspeakable crimes against the Church; through public streets and churches shall blood run, like a rain.

NOSTRADAMUS, EPISTLE TO KING HENRY II OF FRANCE

❉

About the coming of our Lord Jesus Christ, brothers, and our being gathered to him: please do not be too easily thrown into confusion or alarmed by any manifestation of the Spirit or any statement or any letter claiming to come from us, suggesting that the Day of the Lord has already arrived. Never let anyone deceive you in any way.

2 THESSALONIANS

❉

❉

And so the Gods will depart from mankind—a grievous thing!—and only evil angels will remain, who will mingle with men, and drive the poor wretches into all manner of reckless crime, into wars, and robberies, and frauds, and all things hostile to the nature of the soul.

HERMES TRISMEGISTUS

The body without a soul shall no longer be sacrificed
On the day of its death shall it be reborn
The divine spirit shall make the soul exult
By seeing the eternal world.

NOSTRADAMUS II, 13

A new law shall occupy a new country
Around Syria, Judaea, and Palestine
The great Barbarian Empire shall crumble
Before the sun's century has finished her course.

NOSTRADAMUS III, 97

The Moorish Law shall seemingly fail
Another shall rise that seems more seductive
The Dnieper shall fall first
Through gifts and tongues that shall be more appealing.

NOSTRADAMUS III, 95

All religious orders shall be abolished, save for those having the rules of the most rigid and stern institutes of the ancient monks. During these calamities, the Pope will die. Through the death of the Supreme Pontiff will the Church be reduced to tearful anarchy; from three hostile powers three popes will be elected at the same time: one Italian, one German, and one Greek; by force of arms will they be placed on the throne. Human blood will be shed in Italy.

CAPUCHIN FRIAR

These are the evil times, a century full of dangers and calamities. Heresy is everywhere, and the followers of heresy are in power almost everywhere . . . But God will permit a great evil against His Church: Heretics and tyrants will come suddenly and unexpectedly; they will break into the Church . . . They will enter Italy and lay Rome waste; they will burn down churches and destroy everything.

VENERABLE BARTHOLOMEW HOLZHAUSER

The Church will sink deeper until she will at last seem to be extinguished, and the succession of Peter and the other Apostles to have expired. After that she will be victoriously exalted in the sight of all who doubt.

ST. NICHOLAS VON FLÜE

Write to your brothers across the world, informing them it is necessary to bring about a reform of both customs and people themselves. If that is not achieved, the bread of the Divine Word will not be broken among the people.

ST. JOHN BOSCO

A broadsword with a twisted tongue
Shall come to the sanctuary of the gods
He shall open the gates to heretics
And stir up the Church militant.

NOSTRADAMUS VIII, 78

From the country of Arabia Felix
Will be born one who will be strong in the law of Muhammad
He shall vex the Spanish and seize Granada
And by the sea he will come to the Ligurian nation [Italy].

NOSTRADAMUS V, 55

Beneath the sacred ground shall be heard the faint voice of a woman
A human flame shall shine for the divine voice
The ground shall be stained with blood
And the sacred temples shall be destroyed by the wicked.

NOSTRADAMUS IV, 24

Men will surrender to the spirit of the age. They will say that if they had lived in our day, faith would be simple and easy. But in their day, they will say, things are complex; the Church must be brought up to date and made meaningful to the day's problems. When the Church and the world are one, then those days are at hand.

ST. ANTONY THE ABBOT

During a terrible storm against the Church, all religious orders will be abolished save for two, the Capuchins and Dominicans . . .

SISTER ROSE ASDENTI TAGGIA

The churches are destroyed, ruined from base to steeple, the religious and the consecrated virgins are expelled from their habitations, delivered to insults and bad treatment, and condemned to prison, multitudes of children and young women are torn from the bosom of the Church, their Mother.

POPE PIUS XI

When the persecution against the Church has spread like a wild conflagration, even to regions thought safe, then the Lord—who knows how to draw glory from all things—will command suddenly the mighty fire and Satan to cease. Then will come universal peace.

JANE LE ROYER

... the festivals of the Church will not be observed. ... The clergy shall be led into error by the misinterpretation of their reading; the relics of the saints will be considered powerless, every race of mankind will become wicked!

ST. COLUMBKILLE

Religious faith will decline; priests will not be respected; people will be intent only on eating and drinking; there will be many incredibly wealthy people and vast numbers of poor; but this wealth will not long endure, for the red caps [communists] will arise. People will hide in the forests and go into exile.

MATTHEW LANG

The holy people of God and keepers of His Law, with the orders of religion, shall be horribly persecuted and troubled so that the blood of clerics shall flow everywhere.

NOSTRADAMUS, EPISTLE TO KING HENRY II OF FRANCE

Two evil influences of Scorpio in conjunction
The great Lord is assassinated in the hall
A new king shall bring a plague to the Church
The heart of Europe dismembered.

NOSTRADAMUS I, 52

Then shall there come a fiercer persecution of the Church than ever.

NOSTRADAMUS, EPISTLE TO KING HENRY II OF FRANCE

Toward the end of the world, there will be a general departure from the Church, most so in obedience to her.

RICHARD ROLLE OF HAMPOLE

The persecution in Italy will begin with the suppression of the Jesuits; they will be restored once more; then a third time will they be suppressed and never restored again.

SISTER ROSE ASDENTI OF TAGGIA

Many sacrifices must be made. Much penance must be done. We must pay many visits to the Blessed Sacrament . . . but first of all we must be very good . . . If we do not do this, punishment awaits us . . . already the cup is filling, and if we do not change we shall be punished.

PROPHECY OF MARY AT GARABANDAL

Space and Extraterrestrials

While interpreters of the prophets are often concerned chiefly with discerning the predictions of the Antichrist, natural disasters, and coming wars, an oft overlooked aspect of prophecy is that of a momentous event coming from beyond the bounds of earth.

Two very different views of these significant events are the collision of the earth with some heavenly body—such as a comet or a meteor—and the arrival of some extrasolar species suddenly and without warning in the skies above humanity's major cities.

It is now known with some certainty that the age of the dinosaurs was ended by the impact of a comet or meteoroid on the surface of the earth with such force that it hurled into the atmosphere enough dust and debris to choke off much of the planet's life. While the possibility of it happening again soon seems remote to the average person, it might be useful to consider a few galactic facts. The earth is way overdue for an impact with something (we are hit by something very big every million years or so), and there are thought to be a trillion comets concentrated beyond Pluto in what is called the Oort Comet Cloud. These comets are sent on their merry and potentially lethal way by passing bodies (such as meteors) or even stars. A thousand comets are known and followed by astronomers, with a dozen spotted each year. Joining comets as possible causes of destruction are the meteors, vast themselves in number, roaming around the solar system. It would take only one sizable comet or meteor to change human history. If this were not disturbing enough, it should be remembered that at any given moment the sum total of people peering into the sky searching for a most unwelcome visitor is fewer than the staff of your local McDonald's—and the scientists and students there earn about as much.

Throughout history, comets and meteors have captured the imaginations and the fear of prophets, being mentioned specifically by such seers as St. Hildegard of Bingen, Mother Shipton, and Nostradamus. Other prophets foretell of a burning sky, a light in the heavens, and a great day of light. Some prophets interpret comets as harbingers of doom, hurling angrily across the horizon and leaving in their wake war and death. Some prophets, like Hildegard, see them as weapons of holy vengeance, coming to inflict the divine wrath upon a sinful world.

Quite different from comets and meteors is the possibility that from the heavens will descend extrasolar life. It is hoped by many that extraterrestrials actually coming to earth will signal the dawn of a glorious new age of peace and happiness. Certainly the day of their coming will be one of the most important in all of history. Another interpretation of the arrival of aliens is less optimistic. As seen in films and novels for nearly a century, an alien invasion (especially as forecast in H.G. Wells's *War of the Worlds* and the films *Invasion of the Body Snatchers, Starship Troopers,* and *Independence Day*) would change everything for humanity, from the possible enslavement of earthlings to an alien overlord to humans ending up as the main course for an extremely hungry group of extraterrestrials. Nostradamus makes several possible references to alien extrasolar beings in his quatrains that follow, as does the Prophecy of Mary at La Salette (with its reference to "evil spirits of the air").

There will come in the year 2000 the day of the Lord, who will judge the living and the dead. Stars and comets will fall from the sky and the Earth will be set on fire with lightning; the old Earth will pass away.

PROPHECY OF WARSAW

During the time when the bearded star appears
Three mighty princes will become enemies
The peace on earth shattered from the skies
The Po, Tiber, a serpent cast upon the shore.

NOSTRADAMUS II, 43

. . . I am going to shake
the heavens,
why the earth will reel on its foundations,
under the wrath of Yahweh Sabaoth,
the day when his anger ignites.

BOOK OF ISAIAH

At the climacterical degree of forty-eight
At the termination of Cancer shall come so great a drought
That fish in the sea, river, and lake are boiled hectic
Bearn and Bigore will be in distress from fire in the sky.

NOSTRADAMUS V, 98

PROPHECIES: 2000

A fiery dragon will cross the sky
Six times before this earth shall die
Mankind will tremble and frightened be
for the sixth heralds in this prophecy.
For seven days and seven nights
Man will watch this awesome sight.

MOTHER SHIPTON

There is coming the great moment of a great day of light. The consciences of this beloved people must be violently shaken so that they may "put their house in order" and offer to Jesus the just reparation for the daily infidelities that are committed on the part of sinners . . .

PROPHECY OF MARY AT FÁTIMA

Come near and listen, you nations, pay attention, you peoples. Let the earth and its contents listen, the world and its entire population. For Yahweh is angry with all the nations, enraged with all their hordes. He has vowed them to destruction, handed them over to slaughter. Their dead will be thrown away, the stench will rise from their corpses, the mountains will run with their blood, the entire array of heaven will fall apart. The heavens will be rolled up like a scroll and all their array will fade away, to fade the leaves falling from the vine.

THE BOOK OF ISAIAH

The Warning is something that is seen in the air, everywhere in the world and is immediately transmitted into the interior of our souls. It will last a very little time, but it will seem a very long time because of its effect within us.

PROPHECY OF MARY AT GARABANDAL

Near Auch, Lectoure and Mirande
A great fire shall fall from the sky for three nights
The cause shall be wonderful and stupendous
And soon after shall come an earthquake.

NOSTRADAMUS I, 46.

In the sky will appear a new sun, blue in color and ten times brighter in the nighttime than any star or planet presently seen from earth. The new star will first be seen before the end of the century.

GORDON MICHAEL SCALLION (ATTRIBUTED)

After terrible suffering for humankind, comes an even greater misery
As the cycle of the century is renewed
Rain, blood, milk famine, sword and plague
In the sky shall be seen a fire, with a long tail of sparks.

NOSTRADAMUS II, 46

Before the comet comes, many nations, the good excepted, will be
scourged by want and famine. The great nation in the ocean that is
inhabited by people of different tribes and descent will be
devastated by earthquake, storm, and tidal wave. It will be divided
and, in great part, submerged. That nation will also have many
misfortunes at sea and lose its colonies.

St. Hildegard of Bingen

Through its tremendous pressure, the comet will blast much out of
the ocean and flood many countries, causing much need and many
plagues. All sea coasts will be full of dread and many will be
destroyed by tidal waves and most living things will be killed—even
those who escape will die from horrible epidemics.

St. Hildegard of Bingen

When a man walks upon the lamp of the night [the Moon], Islam
shall fall.

The Prophet Muhammad

Upon people and beasts shall come a horrible destruction
Vengeance will be seen suddenly
Blood, hand, thirst, famine, when the comet passes.

Nostradamus II, 62

All states will be shaken by war and civil conflict. During a darkness lasting three days the people given to evil ways will perish so that only one-fourth of mankind will survive.

SR. MARY OF JESUS CRUCIFIED OF PAU

✦

... the sun will be darkened, the moon will not give its lights, the stars will fall from the sky and the powers of the heavens will be shaken.

GOSPEL OF MATTHEW

✦

There shall be wonders and strange appearances in heaven and on earth before the end of the world come.

APOCALYPSE OF THOMAS

✦

There will be signs in the sun and moon and stars; on earth nations in agony, bewildered by the turmoil of the ocean and its waves; men fainting with terror and fear at what menaces the world, for the powers of heaven will be shaken.

GOSPEL OF LUKE

✦

Evil spirits of the air will bring forth strange things upon the Earth and will throw men into destruction.

PROPHECY OF MARY AT LA SALETTE

✦

✦

Fire from the sky to the earth, the color of gold shall be seen.
Struck of the high born one, a marvelous event
Great massacre of humanity, a nephew seized from the great one
The proud one escapes as the dead look on.

NOSTRADAMUS II, 92

And when the dragon's tail is gone,
Man forgets, and smiles, and carries on
To apply himself—too late, too late
For mankind has earned deserved fate.
His masked smile—his false grandeur,
Will serve the Gods their anger stir.
And they will send the Dragon back
To light the sky—his tail will crack
Upon the earth and rend the earth
And man shall flee, King, Lord, and serf.

MOTHER SHIPTON

The warning comes directly from God and will be visible to the
whole world and from any place where anyone may happen to be. It
will be like the revelation of our sins and it will be seen and felt by
everyone, believer and unbeliever alike irrespective of whatever
religion he may belong to. It will be seen and felt in all parts of the
world and by every person.

PROPHECY OF MARY AT GARABANDAL

COMETS: THE DRAGON'S TAIL

Mother Shipton used the colorful description of the Dragon's Tail to signify a comet that will bring terror to the world. She has been joined in her portrait by the Babylonians (who called comets "beards in the heavens"), Greeks, Chinese, and Arabs, all of whom had very colorful terms for the irregular visitors to our part of the Milky Way. Appearing suddenly and often without explanation, comets have long been causes of panic, awe, terror, and religious fervor, being misinterpreted as portents of some imminent doom for the world or signaling a colossal happening in human affairs. A Lutheran bishop in Magdeburg named Andreas Celichius once explained that comets were the result of humanity's sins "rising every day, every hour, every moment, full of stink and horror before the face of God, and becoming slowly so dense as to form a comet." The waggish reply often given to the cheerless bishop was that if comets were made by sin, the heavens would be choked full of them!

The most famous comet, of course, is Halley's, named in honor of Sir Edmund Halley who, in 1707, calculated correctly that the comet would return every seventy-six years to dazzle the world. The comet's timing has been, at times, quite impeccable for those who see them as omens for the future. It blazed across the heavens in A.D. 66 (noted by the historian Josephus), a mere four years before the destruction of Jerusalem by the Romans; in 1066 it was witnessed by the Normans (and seen in the famed Bayeux Tapestry) before they invaded England; in 1912, it caused considerable panic—people actually wore gas masks to be saved from the comet's presumed poison vapors— little knowing what would befall the globe only two years later.

Recently, the two comets attracting the most notoriety were Comet Hyakutake and Comet Hale-Bopp. Hyakutake passed what astronomers call a dangerously close 76 million miles from the earth, while in 1997, Hale-Bopp provided a spectacular light show and ample demonstration that comets have lost none of their hold over the fears, superstitions, and hysteria of humans. Convinced that a spaceship awaited them behind the comet, members of the Heaven's Gate cult killed themselves in a macabre ritual suicide luridly captured on a video camera by other members who then calmly killed themselves after insuring that the remains of their fellows were fully prepared for the expected journey. Hale-Bopp, too, has been seen by others— who did not go so far as to kill themselves—as a harbinger of war and chaos in the last years of the millennium.

And those that live will ever fear
The dragons tail for many year
But time erases memory
You think it strange. But it will be.

MOTHER SHIPTON

There will come three days of darkness, during which the atmosphere will be infected by innumerable devils who will bring the death of large multitudes . . .

PALMA MARIA D'ORIA

Now I will tell of a very evident sign, that you may understand when the end of all things is coming . . . When swords in the starlit heaven appear by night towards dusk and towards dawn, and straightway dust is carried from heaven to earth, and all the brightness of the sun fails at midday from the heavens, and the moon's rays shine forth and come back to earth, and a sign comes from the rock with dripping streams of blood . . .

SIBYLLINE ORACLES

God will ordain two punishments: One, in the form of wars, revolutions and other evils, will originate on earth; the other will be sent from heaven. There shall come over the whole of the earth three days of intense darkness that will last for three days and three nights. Nothing will be visible and the air will be heavy with pestilence . . . During this darkness artificial light will be impossible. Only blessed candles can be lighted. Any who look out a window or leave their house will fall dead.

BLESSED ANNA MARIA TAIGI

In the year 1999 and seven months
From the sky shall come the great King of Terror
He shall resurrect the leader of the Mongols
Before and after Mars shall reign happily.

NOSTRADAMUS X, 72

But not on land already there
But on ocean beds, stark, dry and bare
Not every soul on Earth will die
As the dragons tail goes sweeping by.

MOTHER SHIPTON

Then the sun shall shine forth suddenly by night and the moon by day; and blood shall trickle forth from wood, and the stone utters its voice: The people shall be in commotion, the outgoings of the stars shall change.

BOOK OF EZEKIEL

Look, the Day of Yahweh is coming, merciless, with wrath and
    burning anger,
to reduce the country to a desert and root out the sinners from it.
For in the sky the stars and Orion will shed their light no longer,
the sun will be dark when it rises, and the moon will no longer give
    its light.

BOOK OF ISAIAH

The heaven shall be moved, the stars shall fall upon the earth, the sun shall be cut in half like the moon, and the moon shall not give her light.

APOCALYPSE OF THOMAS

PART TWO

PROPHECIES OF HOPE

> *The "old" is about to give birth to the "new."*
> COUNT LOUIS HAMON (CHEIRO)

It seems at times that the prophets and seers are capable only of seeing death and destruction, plagues and war, ruin and suffering. Fortunately for the earth's inhabitants—especially if even a small portion of the predictions are proven to be correct—there are many prophecies of hope and promise. The prophets foretell of changes in society, an end of war, and, above all, a maturation of the spirit and a transformation of the human consciousness.

Madame Helena Blavatsky, Cheiro, and others see a "new" world in which the "old" order has been swept away to be replaced by "an age of light." Madame Blavatsky saw this not only as a new era of peace and spiritual unity, but a literal evolution of the human race, manifested in the birth of a different and superior generation of evolved humans. Others prefer to interpret scriptural prophecies and the seers in a more eschatological fashion. They see the coming years as the End Times, connecting the rise of the Antichrist and the bloody wars of 1999–2000 with the Second Coming of Christ and the Last Judgment. After the defeat of Satan by the forces of Light, there will come the "new Jerusalem" and a Golden Age of peace. The seer Max Toth saw the Second Coming in 2025 not as a glorious return from the Heavens but as a Second Incarnation of the Messiah, followed by other Messianic Incarnations culminating in the Grand Climacteric of 6300 (see also appendix for dates of the end of the world). The return of the Lord is also seemingly confirmed by Nostradamus through several quatrains, including the lovely one about the "coming of the great lawgiver," although some interpreters have taken this to be a reference to the American president Abraham Lincoln, the emancipator of the slaves in the United States.

Cheiro saw quite correctly the greater role and significance of women in the world. His vision of the ascendancy of women has been fulfilled through their far greater role in power sharing than was the case in the early twentieth century (when Cheiro made his predictions) and the election of women as leaders in countries all over the world, including Great Britain, Ireland, India, Turkey, the Philippines, Canada, and the United States. Indeed, it is hardly a momentous prediction today that a woman will be elected president of the United States in the next years.

Aside from peace, social progress, and greater spiritual depth for humanity, the next years may witness continued advances in space travel, medicine, transportation, and technology. It can be deduced that much of the progress will come from America and Russia. Both Cheiro and Edgar Cayce see the one-time Soviet Empire being changed so profoundly that Russia comes, as Cayce put it, to be "the hope of the world." Such might be the power of prayer and the movement of history.

The day will come when Russian waste of blood—the blood she has and will yet pour out like water—will make "a new heaven and a new Earth . . ."

COUNT LOUIS HAMON (CHEIRO)

In all lands, in all peoples, the "travail pains" are becoming more and more intense . . . Alas, to those who must cling to the "old"; to the traditions of the past, to the habits of their forebears;—their day has already passed forever. The clock of Time has struck the "Midnight Hour"; the blackest darkness lies before the greatest dawn.

COUNT LOUIS HAMON (CHEIRO)

The sacred pomp shall bow down her wings
At the coming of the great law giver
He shall raise up the humble and vex the rebellious
No rival shall be born on earth.

NOSTRADAMUS V, 79

Then I saw *a new heaven and a new earth;* the first heaven and the first earth had disappeared now, and there was no longer any sea. I saw the holy city, and the new Jerusalem, coming down from God out of heaven, as beautiful as a bride all dressed for her husband. Then I heard a loud voice call from the throne, "You see this city. Here God lives among men. He will make *his home among them; they will be his people;* and he will be their God; His name is *God-with-them. He will wipe* away all *tears from their eyes;* there will be no more death, and no more mourning or sadness. The world of the past has gone."

BOOK OF REVELATION

Through Russia comes the hope of the world. Not in respect to what is sometimes termed Communism or Bolshevism. No. But freedom, freedom! That each man will live for his fellow man. The principle has been born there. It will take years for it to be crystallized. Yet out of Russia comes again the hope of the world.

EDGAR CAYCE

And before the race is built anew
A silver serpent comes to view
And spew out men of like unknown
To mingle with the earth now grown
Cold from its heat and these men can
Enlighten the minds of future man.
To intermingle and show them how
To live and love and thus endow
The children with the second sight.
A natural thing so that they might
Grow graceful, humble and when they do
The Golden Age will start anew.

MOTHER SHIPTON

And then they will see the Son of Man coming in the clouds with great power and glory. And then he will send the angels to gather his elect from the four winds, from the ends of the world to the ends of the sky.

GOSPEL OF MARK

PROPHECIES: 2000

Peace, union, and change shall come
Estates, offices, the low shall be high and the high low
The first child prepares for a journey
War shall cease, with civil processes and discord.

NOSTRADAMUS IX, 66

❊

... Women have to come to the front in all matters of public life. I
have no hesitation in saying that there is no body of men who will
be able for long to resist the tide of thought for either good or evil
that is bringing women into power.

COUNT LOUIS HAMON (CHEIRO)

❊

At the signal given by the voice of the Archangel and the trumpet of
God, the Lord himself will come down from heaven; those who
have died in Christ will be the first to rise, and only after that shall
we who remain alive be taken up in the clouds, together with them,
to meet the Lord in the air.

I THESSALONIANS

❊

But the land that rises from the sea
Will be dry and clean and soft and free
Of mankind's dirt and therefore be
The source of man's new dynasty.

MOTHER SHIPTON

❊

❊

After this [misery] has endured a time, there shall be reborn the reign of Saturn and a golden age. God the Creator shall declare—after hearing the lamentation of His people—Satan to be put away and consigned to the depths; there shall begin an age of universal peace between God and man. The power of the Church shall return in full vigor and Satan shall be bound for 1000 years . . .

NOSTRADAMUS, EPISTLE TO KING HENRY II OF FRANCE

We are at the close of the cycle of 5,000 years of the present Aryan Kali Yuga or dark age. This will be succeeded by an age of light. Even now under our very eyes, the new Race or Races are preparing to be formed, and that is in America that the transformation will take place, and has already silently commenced. This Race will be altered in mentality and will move toward a more perfect spiritual existence.

MADAME HELENA BLAVATSKY

Through intense tribulation shall man be brought nearer to perfection and more fitted to enjoy the wonders of the new Aquarian Age, that, born in the blood and sacrifice, will in the end fulfill the meaning of its symbol "the Water Bearer," whose pouring out of water on the earth is the emblem of unselfishness—the negation of Self—arrived at through suffering.

COUNT LOUIS HAMON (CHEIRO)

. . . Yahweh my God will come, and all the holy ones with him. That Day, there will be no light, but only cold and frost. And it will be one continuous day—Yahweh knows—there will be no more day and night, and it will remain light right into the time of evening. When that Day comes, living waters will issue from Jerusalem, half towards the eastern sea, half towards the western sea; they will flow summer and winter. The Yahweh will become king of the whole world.

BOOK OF ZECHARIAH

There shall be signs of the sun and moon when there shall be created a man stronger than any prince, and he shall renew the face of the Church. At this time, the Antichrist will have been trodden under foot and all the world will embrace the faith and the peace of the Lord.

ST. JOHN CAPISTRANO

Women throughout the world will enjoy increased opportunities and privileges. Along with this new freedom will come social tolerance of sexual conduct formerly condoned only in men. In addition, because of the greater availability of jobs, more women will choose not to have children.

COUNT LOUIS HAMON (CHEIRO)

The wall shall be transformed from brick to marble
For seventy-five years there shall be peace
Happiness to the people, the waterway shall be rebuilt
Health, abundance of fruit, joy, and mellifluous times.

NOSTRADAMUS X, 89

Around the world men's thoughts will fly
Quick as the twinkling of an eye.
And water shall great wonders do
How strange. And yet it shall come true.
Through towering hills proud men shall ride
No horse or ass move by his side.
Beneath the water, men shall walk
Shall ride, shall sleep, shall even talk.
And in the air men shall be seen
In white and black and even green.

MOTHER SHIPTON

He shall come to take himself to the corner of Luna
Where he will be taken and placed in a strange place.
The green fruit shall be in some disarray
A great shame, praise to another.

NOSTRADAMUS IX, 65

When everything has been ruined by war; when Catholics are hard pressed by traitorous co-religionists and heretics; when the Church and her servants are denied their rights, the monarchies have been abolished and their rulers murdered . . . then Almighty God will bring a marvelous change, something apparently impossible to human understanding.

VENERABLE BARTHOLOMEW HOLZHAUSER

It may be that the revolution and upheavals we see around us on all sides may for the time being bring about the fall of Empires, the destruction of Thrones, the death of the "old" and the birth of the "new." It may be that times of great tribulations lie in store for humanity—I am, however, such a believer in the ultimate perfection of divine Design that I see in the symbol of the Aquarian Age the promise of "the Water Bearer" pouring out water on the earth, that in the end seeds may have more richness, flowers more fullness, and all sections of humanity more love for one another.

COUNT LOUIS HAMON (CHEIRO)

SELIN, king, Italy shall be in peace
The kingdoms shall be united by a Christian king of the world.
At his death he shall desire to be buried in sacred earth
After driving the pirates from the sea.

NOSTRADAMUS IV, 77

Following the birth of the Antichrist, the people of the earth will be very wicked and godless . . . the religious will crave for worldly things. The churches will be dreary and empty like deserted barns . . . subjects will be oppressed by monarchs and officials. From the midst of His Church He will raise up a Christian ruler who will perform most remarkable deeds. With divine aid, this king will not only bring erring souls back to the true faith but also deal a heavy blow to the foes of the empire.

DIONYSIUS OF LUXEMBOURG

. . . the peculiar children who will grow into peculiar men and women—will be regarded as abnormal oddities, physically and mentally. Then as they increase, and the numbers become with every age greater, one day they will awake to find themselves in a majority. Then present men will begin to be regarded as exceptional mongrels, until they die out in their turn in civilized lands.

MADAME HELENA BLAVATSKY

And in some far off distant land
Some men—oh such a tiny band
Will have to leave their solid mount
And span the earth, those few to count,
Who survives this (unreadable) and then
Begin the human race again.

MOTHER SHIPTON

PROPHECIES: 2000

The scourge being extinguished
The world becomes smaller and lands shall be inhabited peacefully
Everyone shall travel safely by land, air, and sea
Then wars shall start up once more.

NOSTRADAMUS I, 63

❈

And now I saw heaven open, and a white horse appear; its rider was called Faithful and True; he is *a judge with integrity*, a warrior for justice. His eyes were flames of fire, and his head was crowned with many coronets; the name written on him was known only to himself, *his cloak was soaked in blood.* He is known by the name, The Word of God. Behind him, dressed in linen of dazzling white, rode the armies of heaven on white horses.

BOOK OF REVELATION

❈

A great man then, shall come and go
For prophecy declares it so.
In water, iron, then shall float
As easy as a wooden boat
Gold shall be seen in stream and stone
In land that is yet unknown.

MOTHER SHIPTON

❈

❈

When twenty years of the reign shall have passed
For seven thousand years another shall take his reign
When the weary Sun resumes his cycle
My prophecy ends and is fulfilled.

NOSTRADAMUS I, 48

APPENDICES

APPENDIX ONE
✝HE PROPHE✝S

The following are the most significant and better known prophets. They vary from saints and popes of the Catholic Church to spiritualists, seers, witches, prognosticators, and half-demons, to the so-called King of the Prophets, Michel de Nostradamus. There are also the prophecies made during the apparitions (or appearances) of the Virgin Mary around the world, and ancient writings—such as the *Mahabharata* and the Sibylline Oracles—that may speak directly from the past to the modern world.

Bacon, Roger (d. 1294): English scientist, philosopher, teacher, and Franciscan friar, considered one of the most learned figures of the Middle Ages. After studying at Oxford, he traveled to Paris, taught the philosophy of Aristotle, and joined the Franciscans around 1251. He spent the next years conducting scientific experiments and studying alchemy, languages, mathematics, and optics. Bacon soon encountered difficulties with Church authorities and was for a time actually imprisoned. A legendary master of learning, he supposedly invented or envisioned telescopes, gunpowder, flying machines, and automobiles. For his vast erudition, he was called the *Doctor Mirabilis* (Amazing Doctor).

Becket, Thomas (d. 1170): Famous martyr, archbishop of Canterbury, and saint. A close associate of King Henry II of England, Becket was named by the ruler to the office of archbishop of Canterbury in the hopes of the crown controlling the Church in the kingdom. Becket, however, underwent a personal conversion and opposed the many schemes of King Henry. After returning from a long exile from England, Becket was murdered by four of Henry's knights while praying in Canterbury Cathedral. His tomb soon became a favorite place of pilgrimage.

Blavatsky, Helena (1831–1891): Famed spiritualist author and one of the founders of the occult organization called the Theosophical Society. Born Helena Hahn, she wed (around 1848) a Russian military officer named Blavatsky, but left him after several months and began a series of travels that lasted for twenty years. During her travels she reportedly studied esoteric Eastern mysticism and religions, using her studies as the basis for the Theosophical movement she began in 1858 in Russia. She later (around 1873) launched the more developed Theosophical Society with Col. H. S. Olcott, with the aim of studying a vast occult system derived from Hindu, ancient Egyptian, and assorted esoteric writings. One of the best known and certainly most flamboyant occult leaders of the nineteenth century, she was the author of such popular and controversial writings as *Isis Unveiled* (1877) and *The Secret Doctrine* (1888). The latter contained prophecies of the future.

Bosco, John (1815–1888): Catholic priest, founder, and saint. A native of Piedmont, Italy, he desired from his youth to become a priest, receiving ordination in 1841. With the aid of his mother, he opened a boarding school for children, laying the foundation for the congregation that was called the Salesians (after St. Francis de Sales). The congregation grew, before his death, to include over one thousand priests and nine hundred sisters. In 1874, he sent a letter to Pope Pius IX that detailed his visions of the future. Still supposedly filed away in the Vatican Secret Archives, the letter presents a dark forecast of things to come for the Church.

Bouquillon, Bertine: A French nun of the nineteenth century who worked in the hospital of St. Louis in St. Omer, France. She predicted the rise of the Antichrist and the coming of the Apocalypse in the late twentieth century.

Brahan the Seer (fl. seventeenth century): A Scottish prophet, known also as Coinneach Odhar Fiossaiche, he was one of the most respected seers among the Highland Scots. Originally known only on his native island of Lewis, his fame soon spread and this simple, humbly dressed farmhand was called upon by the most powerful clan leaders in Scotland. Using a polished blue stone or piece of meteor, he gave uncannily accurate predictions to his patrons, as well as broad visions of the far future, relating mainly to Scotland. Brahan was put to death by being plunged head first into a barrel of burning tar with spikes on the inside after giving a prediction, called the Doom of the Seaforths, to the easily enraged Countess of Seaforth who also clearly had a poor sense of perspective. Just before his own death, he hurled his divining stone into a loch, declaring that whoever found it would inherit the gift of divination.

Bufalo, Caspar del (1786–1836): Founder of the Missioners of the Most Precious Blood, a religious congregation devoted to missionary work in Italy with the aim of bolstering the faith there. He suffered during the era of Napoleon Bonaparte in the early 1800s and spent time in exile on Corsica for refusing to swear allegiance to the French emperor. Renowned for his holiness and his visions, he was canonized a saint in 1955.

Caesarius of Arles (d. 542): Archbishop of Arles, in southern France, and a famous preacher. He was responsible for helping to organize the Christian Church in Gaul (France) and authored a directory for monks, a rule for nuns, and perhaps a collection of canons. His prophecies were concerned with the so-called Great Monarch, a virtuous temporal ruler who would give aid to a great pope and ameliorate the sufferings of the Church under the Antichrist.

Capistrano, John (1386–1456): Franciscan friar and preacher. Born in Capistrano, Italy, he served as a governor and spent time as a prisoner of war. During his incarceration, he had a vision of St. Francis and, upon his release, he joined the Franciscans. The next years were spent preaching with great zeal and aiding the besieged city of Belgrade during a bloody invasion by the Ottoman Turks. John made an intriguing prophecy about the last eight pontiffs during the age of tribulations endured by the Church at the hands of the Antichrist.

Capuchin Friar (fl. eighteenth century): A member of the Franciscan Order, of the branch known as the Capuchins, in France. In 1776, this otherwise unknown friar made a dire prediction about the future of the Catholic Church. His most terrible prophecy tells of the election of three popes, thus tearing apart for a time the unity of the faith. He also spoke of the Antichrist (or Mystic Antichrist), whom he called the Emperor of the North.

Cayce, Edgar (1877–1945): The so-called Sleeping Prophet, one of the foremost seers of the modern age who made remarkably accurate predictions concerning the second World War. Born near Hopkinsville, Kentucky, he was a religious youth and was aided early on by a voice that, for example, instructed him in spelling while he slept. Hit in the head during a baseball game, he acquired a remarkable skill in prescribing healing recipes rooted in natural medicine. He also entered into states of deep meditative sleep during which he answered questions from visitors and prescribed assorted cures. His answers were astonishingly accurate and his cures very often yielded nearly miraculous results. In 1927, he settled in Virginia Beach, Virginia, and soon grew in fame, receiving requests for help from all over the world. In 1931, he received a vision of a coming war that would bring the deaths of millions, a global conflict that commenced—as he had predicted—in 1939. Cayce also made predictions for the close of the century, ranging from new wars to wholesale global upheaval through earthquakes, storms, and volcanoes.

Cheiro (1866–1936): The name used by the British palmist, clairvoyant, and seer Count Louis Hamon. An adventurer and entrepreneurial occultist, he worked for the British Secret Service during World War I, was a lover of Mata Hari, and, after moving to Los Angeles, became one of Hollywood's earliest spiritual advisors. Among his clients were Mary Pickford and Lillian Gish. His main prophetic writing was *Cheiro's World Predictions* (1926, revised in 1931), in which he gave his often accurate predictions for the future. His adopted name, Cheiro, was taken from the Greek word meaning "hand."

Chrysostom, John (347–407): Bishop of Constantinople and one of the great theologians in the history of Christianity. Drawn to the religious life but hampered by poor health and his own extreme asceticism, he became a priest and was so brilliant a preacher that he was christened Chrysostom, or "golden-mouthed." Compelled by public demands to accept the post of Bishop of Constantinople, he fell prey to the vicious intrigue of the court of the emperors and was exiled and brutalized until his death. He prophesied about the world at the time of the Antichrist.

Columbkille (d. 597): Also called Columba, Colum, and Columcille, he was one of the most famous saints in Scotland, founding monasteries in Ireland and Scotland. Columbkille is perhaps best known for establishing the renowned monastery of Iona, which served as one of the great centers of learning in the British Isles. He was described as having "the face of an angel." His prophecies—centered on the future of Ireland—included the invasion by the Anglo-Normans from England in the twelfth century and the Irish potato famine of the ninteenth century.

Conan Doyle, Sir Arthur (1859–1930): Creator of Sherlock Holmes and one of the world's most famous mystery writers. A native of Scotland, he studied medicine and, after voyages to West Africa and the Arctic, set himself up in a practice in Southsea, England. To help pass the time when patients were not numerous, Conan Doyle took up writing, eventually selling his first Sherlock Holmes story, "A Study in Scarlet" (1887). After enjoying international success with Holmes (he actually grew so tired of the detective that he tried to kill him off), Conan Doyle developed a passion for spiritualism, authoring some thirty books on the subject and dabbling extensively in seances. He promised to send a message (as yet apparently unreceived) to his loved ones from beyond the grave.

Didache: The earliest known writing of the Christian epoch, outside of the New Testament, the *Didache* offers an abstract of moral teachings. The title is derived from the longer original Greek title of the "Teaching of the Twelve Apostles," and the work (composed around A.D. 60) offers chapters on the Way of Life and the Way of Death, baptism, prayer, the Eucharist, false and true prophets, and a prophecy on the Second Coming of the Lord.

Ferrer, Vincent (d. 1449): Famous Spanish Dominican preacher and prophet. A native of Valencia, he entered the Dominicans in 1367 and studied at Barcelona. From an early age, he displayed a very deep faith, and had visions of Christ, St. Francis of Assisi, and St. Dominic. On the basis of these, he became a brilliant preacher, traveling across Europe and speaking before huge crowds. Vincent also was gifted with the skills of a seer, predicting accurately the arrival of grain ships to end a famine. He predicted the coming of a false prophet, the predecessor of the Antichrist.

Fiore, Joachim da (c. 1132–1202): Mystic and apocalyptic writer and visionary. Born in Italy, he went on a pilgrimage to the Holy Land as a young man and, upon his return to Italy, entered the Cistercian order. After serving as an abbot, he resigned and devoted himself to a contemplative life and writing. Before his death, he founded a small community that became the Order of San Giovanni in Fiore. His writings were heavily apocalyptic, elaborating upon the theme of history existing in three stages. The last age, that of the Holy Spirit, would culminate in the conversion of the entire world, but not before a time of intense suffering for the Church and believers.

Flüe, Nicholas von (1417–1487): Swiss mystic and saint, known as Brother Klaus. A native of Lake Lucerne, he fought in several wars and raised a family before giving up all material interests in 1467 to become a hermit. His wisdom and goodness made him a much sought after advisor to the mighty and the humble alike. His prophecy is a dark one for the Church, but one that is not without hope.

Genet, Brother (fl. eighteenth century): French abbot of the monastery of Clarisses, in Brittany, France. He made assorted prophecies, especially about the twentieth century, which he saw as a dark time, culminating before its end with the Second Coming of Christ.

Gurdjieff, George Izanovich (1866–1949): Noted spiritualist, psychologist, and one of the twentieth century's most famous experts on religion. Born in the Russian Caucasus, he set out at a young age upon a twenty-year voyage of discovery through Tibet, the Far East, and the Holy Land to study aspects of religion and esoteric belief. His journey was similar to that of other late-nineteenth-century occultists and sparked a lifelong interest in philosophy, theology, and religion, as well as dance, medicine, psychology, the Cabala, and science. Returning to Russia, he attracted followers and founded his so-called Mystery School, an enterprise cut short by the Russian revolution of 1917. The school was reopened in France in 1922. His three main works are *Beelzebub's Tales to His Grandson, Meetings with Remarkable Men,* and *Life is Real Only Then When "I Am."*

Hildegard of Bingen (1098–1179): German abbess and mystic, called the Sibyl of the Rhine for her many prophetic visions. One of the great women of the Middle Ages, she experienced visions from an early age and entered the Benedictine order under the influence of the famed recluse Blessed Jutta around 1116. Becoming abbess of a Benedictine community, Hildegard acquired much influence in Germany and was a cordial correspondent with the age's foremost leaders, including popes, kings, and saints. A profound mystic and seer, she compiled her visions into a collection called the *Scivias,* a grim assembly of largely apocalyptic visions. Perhaps her most startling prediction is that of a comet striking the earth.

Holzer, Hans: A prominent parapsychologist who compiled the predictions of British and American seers into a 1971 book entitled *The Prophets Speak.* This work was updated in 1995 to examine the accuracy of the prognostications under the title *Prophecies. Visions of the World's Fate: Truths, Possibilities, or Fallacies.*

Holzhauser, Bartholomew (d. 1658): German priest, writer, and prophet. A native of Augsburg, he was a brilliant student, earning a doctorate in philosophy before ordination as a priest. He labored as a parish priest in Salzburg and Mainz until his death. To help repair the terrible spiritual damage inflicted by the Thirty Years War (1618–1648), Holzhauser founded the so-called Bartholomites, a congregation of priests devoted to revitalizing the life of the faithful. Among his many writings were *Visiones*, a collection of ten prophecies, and *Interpretatio Apocalypsis usque ad cap. XV.v.5*, an interpretation of the Book of Revelation. His visions included the execution of King Charles I of England, the French Revolution, Hitler, and missile warfare.

Hyppolitus (d. 236): Theologian, writer, and an antipope (or illegal claimant to the papacy). A gifted theologian, he opposed several popes by holding different theological positions. He died in exile on Sardinia during the Roman persecutions. The author of numerous works, he penned commentaries on the Old and New Testaments and a treatise on the Antichrist.

Johansson, Anton (1858-1929): Norwegian fisherman and seer. Born in Sweden, he moved to Norway and worked in various areas, such as fishing, teaching, and cartography. At an early age, he demonstrated gifts of prophecy. These allowed him to predict the 1906 San Francisco earthquake and the 1912 sinking of the Titanic. In 1907 he experienced a series of shattering visions concerning the future, including World War I, World War II, and beyond.

Lactantius (c. 245–323): Called in full Lucius Caecilius Firmianus Lactantius, he was a brilliant apologist, or defender of the early Christian faith. Originally a servant of the pagan emperor Diocletian, he was converted to Christianity and enjoyed a favored position under the pro-Christian emperor Constantine the Great

(d. 337), who ended the persecution of the Church. Lactantius authored a large body of works to promote the faith and wrote about the Antichrist, "the overthrower and destroyer of the human race."

Mahabharata: One of the great epics of India, translated as the "great Epic of the Bharata." A poem of nearly 100,000 couplets, the *Mahabharata* tells of the mighty struggle for power between two families, but its primary purpose was to impart essential Hindu teachings. It examines in various ways the dharma (or right action), leading to the overcoming of the cycle of birth, death, and rebirth. Some of its descriptions of war and destruction are strikingly modern and familiar.

Malachy (1049–1148): Archbishop of Arnagh, Ireland, and reputed author of a famous set of prophecies concerning the papacy. Known in Irish as Máel Máedoc Úa Morgair, he was one of the most significant Church leaders in the history of Ireland, although his ecclesiastical labors have long been overshadowed by the renown of the so-called Prophecies of Malachy. While scholars are in general agreement that the prophecies are unconnected with Malachy, beyond their spurious attribution to him, Malachy's name is now inextricably connected to them. The prophecies claim to attach a motto for every pope from Celestine II (r. 1143–1144) to Peter II, or Peter the Roman, who will lead the Church in its last days of tribulation.

Maria Laach Monastery, Prophecy of (sixteenth century): The name given to a set of prophecies preserved in the Maria Laach Monastery in the Rhineland, Germany. They cover future events, including those of the twentieth century.

Marienthal, Prophecy of: A monastery near Strasbourg, Germany, that was originally founded in the thirteenth century and has subsequently survived the many wounds and disasters of war and natural calamities. According to legend, anyone who seeks sanctuary within its walls is able to avoid for a time the fulfillment of his or her fate. The monastery preserves a *Book of Pilgrimage* (c. 1750) that contains a prophecy on the future, including events of the twentieth century.

Mary of the Crucified Jesus of Pau (1846–1878): Also called Marie Baouardy and the Little Arab, she was a nun, mystic, and seer. Born in Abellin, Palestine, she was the only one of fifteen children to survive childhood and was orphaned at the age of three. Raised as a Christian, she entered the Carmelite nuns at Pau, France, and soon demonstrated mystical and prophetic gifts. She later founded a house of Carmelites in Bethlehem and Nazareth, dying in Bethlehem after a fall. She was beatified (the step just below canonization) by Pope John Paul II in 1983.

Merlin (fifteenth century): The most famous of all the prophets of England, Merlin is best known through Arthurian legend and was a reputed sorcerer, the spawn of the devil or some demon. There is a possibility that he actually lived in England during the period after the departure of the Romans in 410. To his name was attached a large body of legends and prophecies. The prophet's predictions are concerned mainly with England and Wales.

Methodius (d. c. 311): Bishop of Lycia (in Asia Minor) and a martyr. He was a prolific author of treatises and hymns; unfortunately only a portion of his writings have survived. His prophecies speak of the end times, when doubt will grip the followers of the Christian faith.

Monk of Padua (fl. eighteenth century): A member of a monastic community in Padua, Italy, who compiled a set of prophecies concerning the last twenty popes before the return of Christ and the

Final Judgment. His predictions mirror closely those of the better known St. Malachy. They attempt a greater specificity, including actual names of the popes; while correct in several instances in the matter of names, the list is out of order and names most of the popes incorrectly.

Neumann, Therese (1898–1962): German mystic and stigmatic. According to accounts from the period, so long as Therese received daily Communion, she required no solid food. A native of Bavaria, she led a normal life until the age of twenty, when she fell ill, went blind, and began to experience visions. She was miraculously cured of her blindness in 1923, and three years later received the stigmata (the signs on the body of the wounds of Christ's Crucifixion). After surviving World War II, she attracted thousands of pilgrims eager to see the wounds of Christ.

Nostradamus (1503–1566): The so-called King of Prophets, whose large collection of prophecies has made him the best known of history's many seers. Also called Michel de Nostradamus and Nostradame, he was born in Saint-Rémy, France, to Jewish converts to Catholicism and studied medicine. After launching his medical practice at Agen in 1529, he moved in 1549 to Salon, Provence, and there acquired a reputation for his skills in healing the victims of plague in Aix and Lyons. Both his abilities as a physician and his notoriety as a prophet brought him to the attention of Catherine de Medici, then queen consort to King Henry II of France. He became her special advisor, predicting accurately (through astrology) the dark and bloody fate of her children; in 1560 he became physician to King Charles IX.

Aside from his medical labors and his consummate skills as an astrologer, Nostradamus earned immortality through his prophecies, organized and published for the first time in 1555 under the title *Centuries*. The prophecies were written in rhymed quatrains and grouped in centuries, or sections of one hundred prophecies. He wrote them in a deliberately obscure style, using an often dizzying variety of languages (including Hebrew, Latin, Greek, Arabic, and French). The obscurity was necessary to avoid as much as possible complications from religious authorities, in particular the Inquisition, which had already hounded him across much of France. A second edition was published in 1558, with a dedication to King Henry II. The introduction itself contains a valuable prophetic letter, offering glimpses of the coming final Antichrist and the Angelic Pastor—a holy pope—who will oppose him. His final three centuries, including some of the most vivid and disturbing prophecies, were published posthumously.

The *Centuries*—as well as his letters to King Henry II and his own son—cover nearly every sphere of human activity, from war and religion to miraculous inventions, political scandals, global travel, natural disasters, and social changes.

His normal method of divination was to retire to his special chambers and peer into a cauldron of water. The *Centuries* have been the source of often intense speculation by analysts and interpreters over the years, with some quatrains seemingly self-evident. Most, however, are exceedingly enigmatic.

Nursing Nun of Belez (d. 1830): A nun in a convent in the French city of Belez. In a vision, she beheld a horrendous struggle facing the Church in the future.

Odilia (d. c. 720): Also Odile and Othilia, the so-called patroness of Alsace and a powerful abbess of the nunnery of Hohenburg (modern Odilienburg). She was the daughter of a Frankish nobleman named Adalricus and was born blind. As Adalricus thought the child cursed, he had her banished to a convent. There she was

miraculously cured. Brought home, she soon found her life spiritu-
ally unappealing and returned to the convent. A developed spiritual
life included visions of the future that were written down before
her death. Through her leadership, the nunnery became a center of
pilgrimage.

Orval, Prophecy of: A prophecy attached to the one-time monastery
of Orval, in Luxembourg, and dated around the thirteenth century.
The monastery was founded in 1071 by Benedictine monks, but in
1132 Cistercian monks took it over. They remained until the
destruction of the monastery in 1793 by forces of the French
Revolution. It is possible that the prophecy was composed in the
thirteenth century by Gilles d'Orval, the only monk of the community to achieve any literary fame.

Pratt, Orson (d. 1881): Mormon leader and writer. Pratt was a store
clerk in Ohio at the time of his conversion to Mormonism by the
faith's founder, Joseph Smith. Subsequently, he was one of the
most active apostles of the Mormon cause, traveling to England
and Scotland and serving as a scout during the great trek of the
Mormons under Brigham Young to Salt Lake, Utah. Later, he
became leader of the Mormon community in England. In his journal, *Orson Pratt, Journal of Discourses,* he recorded his prophecies of a
second American civil war.

Quetzalcoatl: One of the chief gods of the Aztec pantheon, as well as
the Toltec pantheon, he was worshipped as a god of light and peace
and the arts, and as a founder of the civilization of Mexico under a
variety of names. (He was the object of a host of legends [being
worshipped as the plumed serpent], including reigning over his people as an absolute monarch and founder of Mesoamerican astrology.) He departed his kingdom but promised to return, a prophecy
that was initially thought to have been fulfilled with the coming of

the powerful, mysterious, and plumed Spanish conquistadors in 1517, with tragic consequences for the pre-Columbian cultures of the continent. Quetzalcoatl is credited with a variety of prophecies.

Richard Rolle of Hampole (d. 1349): English mystic, poet, and writer. A native of Yorkshire, England, he studied at Oxford and Paris and then embarked upon the life of a hermit, wandering through England before settling finally at Hampole. While never canonized, he was still the object of visitations by pilgrims and his tomb was the supposed site of miracles. He authored numerous treatises on mysticism, as well as poems, and is the supposed recipient of visions of the future.

Scallion, Gordon Michael: Modern American seer and futurist, best known for his predictions of looming natural disasters. An electronics worker, around 1979 he suffered a period of sudden poor health. Surviving the ordeal, he received what he claims are spiritual gifts, including prophecy. Since then, he has supposedly predicted with remarkable accuracy numerous earthquakes and various other events, such as the floods along the Mississippi and Hurricane Andrew. Scallion currently lectures and serves as editor and publisher of the *Earth Changes Report.*

Shipton, Mother (1488–1561): The name generally given to Ursula Southill, a witch from Yorkshire, England, who became one of the best known of English seers. The subject of legend and often wild stories (her mother, Agatha Southill, supposedly was given a child one winter evening by a diabolical visitor who not only sired Ursula but gifted Agatha with certain supernatural powers), she was reputed to possess the abilities of a witch, including that of foresight. Married at twenty-four to Tobias Shipton, she became famous in the area around York for her prophecies. Many were written down, subsequently becoming the basis for

MATTHEW BUNSON

assorted embellishments and outright forgeries. Her prophecies are nevertheless of considerable interest for their imagery and their flamboyant assurances of catastrophe. As for Mother Shipton, she died in her bed in 1561, the year she foretold would see her demise.

Sibylline Oracles: The name used by the Romans for a body of prophecies issued by a group of seers known as the Sibyls (or Sibyllae in the plural). By custom, the first Sibyl was the daughter of Dardanus and Neso who received visions by the will of the god Apollo. She was succeeded by other Sibyls, whose number varied from three, four, and ten, to fourteen. The most famous Sibyl, that of Cumae, Italy, supposedly sold to King Tarquinius Superbus a set of prophetic books that were subsequently consulted by the Roman Senate before undertaking important decisions. The Sibylline Books were eventually burned by the Christian emperor Honorius, although Christian and Jewish versions soon appeared. The Christian version, called the Sibylline Oracles, offered a disturbing set of prophecies.

Stormberger: An eighteenth-century German seer who is respected as one of the most accurate prophets since Nostradamus. A simple farm laborer in Bavaria, he was renowned for his prophecies about the future. With remarkable skill, he predicted the invention of aircraft and automobiles, and stated with exact precision the day on which World War I commenced. He foresaw the Great Depression, World War II, the division of East and West Germany, and a third, truly appalling global war that is soon to come.

Taigi, Anna Maria (d. 1837): Italian peasant girl who was declared Blessed by the Catholic Church (the stage just below canonization as a saint). She received a profound vision of Christ a few years before her death. She was told by the vision that two terrible punishments will befall the world: one in the form of war, the other a dreadful plague coming from the Heavens. Like other prophets, she saw a time of three days of darkness.

Telesphorus of Cosenza (d. 1388): Also called Theophorus, a visionary and self-proclaimed prophet during the late Middle Ages. A popular seer during a period known for its many prophets and prognosticators, Telesphorus compiled the *Liber de magnis tribulationibus in proximo futuris (The Book of Great Tribulations in the Near Future)* around 1386, a book of prophecies related to the Great Schism that was then dividing the Christian Church. It is a striking work for its mention of the "Angelic Pastor," a saintly pontiff who will lead the Church during the troubled time of the Antichrist.

Vatiguerro, João de (fl. thirteenth century): Also John of Vatiguerro, a Christian seer who made a series of terrible prophecies about the future of the papacy, including the apparent flight of the pope from Rome.

Wallraff, Helen (d. 1801): German seer who lived in Cologne. She made predictions about the future of the papacy.

Warsaw, Prophecy of: A prophetic document composed by a Polish monk around 1790 that offers an accurate glimpse into the future. He correctly predicted the Napoleonic Wars, the partition of Poland, and World War II, and predicts the struggles that will close the twentieth century. The Prophecy also mentions the opportunity for peace that began in 1986 with Glasnost in the Soviet Union.

Wittmann, Bishop George Michael (1760-1833): Catholic bishop and author. He was best known for his writings and his many years spent as a professor at the seminary of Ratisbon, Germany. His works included a translation of the New Testament and a treatise on the Pentateuch. During his life, he was known for his zeal and extremely exemplary life.

Young, Brigham (d. 1877): Leader of the Mormon Church (Church of Jesus Christ of the Latter Day Saints) and its most important figure after the martyrdom of its founder, Joseph Smith, in 1844. Brigham Young led the Mormon faithful on its great trek across the West, settling finally at the Great Salt Lake in Utah. In his *Journal of Discourses*, he recorded a set of prophecies about America. He foresaw a time of civil chaos, natural disasters, and social disorder, all before the coming of the twenty-first century.

APPENDIX TWO

BIBLICAL PROPHECIES

The Bible, revered by Christians as Sacred Scripture and the source of revelation, remains one of the deepest wells for prophetic sustenance. Within its long books covering the history of ancient Israel and the founding of the Christian Church is a host of prophetic visions and writings, from the harrowing images of Isaiah and St. John to the promises of the future contained in the four Gospels. The following are the books of the Old and New Testament quoted in this work.

OLD TESTAMENT

Amos: A book concerning the vision of the shepherd Amos, it includes the judgment of the Lord upon Israel and the looming threat of the Assyrians (who invaded in 721 B.C.). Throughout, however, is the promise that a remnant of Israel would survive.

Daniel: A major book of the Old Testament, composed during the time of persecution of the Jews by the Syrian king Antiochus Epiphanes (167-164 B.C.)—one of the models for the Antichrist—Daniel contains some of the most vivid visions in the whole of Scripture. The book is an important source for prophecies concerning the End Times.

Ezekiel: The book devoted to the visions and prophecies of Ezekiel. The work stresses through allegory the central hope that existed for the future of Israel in the Babylonian exiles (at a time when most of the Israelites were in captivity in Babylon) rather than the faithless Jews who remained in conquered Jerusalem.

Isaiah: One of the greatest compilations of the Jewish prophets, Isaiah offers prophecies concerning the future of Israel and the coming of one who will bring salvation through the sacrifices of himself. Above all, Isaiah stresses the place of Israel in the hands of God.

Joel: A book with two themes. The first is a call to repentance, with the powerful image of a plague of locusts. The second is a promise of salvation and hope for the world.

Psalms: One of the most beloved books of the Old Testament, the book of Psalms offers a vast collection of hymns and prayers for virtually every situation, from victory and defeat to joy and sorrow.

Zechariah: One of the prophetic books of the Old Testament, it has two main parts. The first is a collection of eight symbolic prophecies and the second is an account of hope concerning the messiah that was written about two centuries after the time of Zechariah (in the sixth century B.C.).

Zephaniah: A prophetic book attributed to Zephaniah (seventh century B.C.), who makes prophecies of the so-called Day of the Lord, a time of great punishment that will leave only a remnant of the faithful.

NEW TESTAMENT

Luke, Gospel of: The third of the synoptic Gospels, Luke focuses on Christ's call to all—both Jew and Gentile—to share in salvation, to embrace the Christian life, and to acknowledge him as the fulfillment of the Old Testament.

Mark, Gospel of: Perhaps the earliest of the Gospels, Mark empha-
sizes the Passion of Christ; it offers proof of Christ's place as the
Messiah and then presents in great detail his Crucifixion and death.

Matthew, Gospel of: One of the three Synoptic Gospels (with Mark
and Luke), Matthew stresses the profound kingship of Jesus, the
formation of the community of believers, and the fulfillment in
Christ of the Old Testament's hopes for the Messiah.

1 John: The first of the three letters of St. John, this epistle is well-
known for its mention of the Antichrist and its warning for
Christians to be alert to false teachers, or false Christs, who would
come at the end of the world.

1 and 2 Thessalonians: Two letters of St. Paul addressed to the
Christians of Thessalonica, these works are famous in the world of
prophecy for their proclamation of the imminent return of Christ.
Paul, however, uses the second letter to caution the enthusiastic
Thessalonians that the time was not yet ripe, but that God's judg-
ment will come suddenly and unexpectedly.

Revelation: One of the most famous books of the New Testament
and perhaps the single most widely read book in the whole realm
of prophecy, Revelation was written probably by St. John the
Evangelist while in exile on the island of Patmos. The work presents extremely striking and often highly enigmatic imagery concerning the end of the world, the persecution of the Church, and
the final, triumphant return of Christ. Prophets and biblical
experts have long struggled to render the prophecies into literal
events and to attach the narrative to their own era, thus far with little success.

Apocryphal Writings

There are several works quoted in this collection that are part of what is known as apocryphal literature—books that are not accepted as genuine Scripture but that still attracted readers and many believers over the ages. Apocryphal writings are often attributed to some famous patriarch (such as Enoch) or a famous apostle (such as Andrew or Peter); they are also often full of intense imagery, apocalyptic themes, and grim forecasts for humanity. Among the apocryphal books quoted are the Books of Enoch and Zephiel, the Revelation of Esdras, and the Apocalypses of Andrew and Peter.

Marian Apparitions

There have been many appearances of the Blessed Virgin Mary over the last few centuries, including Lourdes, Fátima, Guadalupe, Knock, and elsewhere. These apparitions have received formal approval by the Catholic Church. The unapproved apparitions—in particular those of Garabandal and Bayside, New York—are accompanied by often hair-raising prophecies of destruction and anarchy should the world fail to heed the Virgin's call for prayer, conversion, and penance. Two of the accepted apparitions—at La Salette and Fátima—also include prophetic promises.

La Salette (1846): A young girl named Mélanie Calvat, the daughter of a stonemason, beheld the Virgin at La Salette, near Grenoble, France, on September 19, 1846. The beautiful lady, as she was described by young Calvat, condemned and expressed lament over the faithless world. Our Lady predicted grave trials for the Church, bloody wars, and global destruction from natural and manmade disasters should there be no repentance.

Fátima (1917): The most famous Marian Apparition (save for Guadalupe and Lourdes), Our Lady appeared at Fátima, north of Lisbon, Portugal, six times between May 13 and October 13; her final visit was observed by 70,000 people and was marked by a miraculous solar phenomenon. She appeared to three children, Lucia dos Santos and her cousins Francisco Marto and Jacinto, in a field and called upon the faithful to pray, do penance, beseech

God for the conversion of Russia, and build a church in her honor. Should all of her requests be followed, world peace would be achieved. She made three prophecies, two of which are known and have been fulfilled. The third—the most famous and apparently disturbing—has never been divulged to the public. It was given to Lucia who wrote it down and sent it to the pope through the bishop of Leiria. It has been read by successive popes and is kept in the Secret Vatican Archives, despite the Lady's request that it be made known in 1960. It is guessed that the third secret of Fátima contains a dire promise of terrible chastisement for the Church in the coming years. A German newpaper, the *Neues Europa,* published what it claimed was a copy of the secret in 1963. The text spoke of cardinals opposing cardinals and Satan walking amongst them, leading to the darkest hour in the history of the Church.

Garabandal (1961–1965): A well-known apparition (as yet unapproved by the Catholic Church) that supposedly took place in the small Spanish town of Garabandal. The Virgin appeared to four children who underwent a series of ecstasies and received several promises from Mary to the world. The Virgin promised a great miracle, a global warning of truly shattering dimensions, and, should there still be no repentance, a dreadful time of suffering.

PROPHECIES OF THE POPES

A number of popes have received visions or prophetic dreams, such as Pope Innocent III (r. 1198–1216), who dreamed of St. Francis of Assisi before actually meeting him. Several pontiffs have also received prophetic visions of a far less serene nature. Pope St. Gregory I the Great (r. 599-604) beheld the Antichrist and the travails to be suffered by the Church. Pope St. Pius X (r. 1903-1914) was granted a harrowing vision of a future pope fleeing Rome by stepping over the corpses of his priests. Pope Pius XI (r. 1922-1939) saw churches destroyed and the faithful terrorized. Pope Pius XII (r. 1939–1958), whose reign came during World War II, had several mystical experiences, although he was reluctant to speak of them. Finally, Pope Leo XIII (1878–1903) was granted a vision of St. Michael defeating Satan and driving him back into Hell. In its honor—and in response to the terrifying nature of the vision—the pope ordered a special prayer recited after each Mass in honor of St. Michael. It was said until the reforms of Vatican Council II (1962–1965).

The End of the World

One of the favorite pastimes of seers, prophets, and religious zealots has been attempting to pinpoint the exact date for the end of the world. Many early Christians hoped for the end to come in their lifetimes, believing firmly that Christ was soon to return. Centuries later, in 999, believers looked upon the new millennium as the coming of the Golden Age of Christ's Kingdom on earth. Both groups of Christians, separated by nearly a thousand years, were to be disappointed.

Perhaps the most famous incorrect stab at the end times was made by the nineteenth-century Seventh Day Adventist William Miller. Using an overly convoluted method of calculation based on passages in the Book of Daniel, he decided that the Second Coming would take place in 1843. There were many who found his arcane mathematics perfectly logical, and Miller soon attracted thousands of followers. When the great day came and the trumpet blast of Gabriel did not resound, Miller announced he had made a slight error in his calculations. The *real* date, he assured his still-gullible disciples, was October 22, 1844. They all gathered anew on the appointed date, only to be frustrated beyond words. Seventh Day Adventists still refer to the event as the "Great Disappointment."

The following is a list of predictions of the date for the end of the world. Those of note are by Morton Edgar (who used the measurements of the Grand Gallery of the Great Pyramid and the estimate of the famous Archishop Ussher, who placed the creation of the world at 4004 B.C.); Max Toth (who predicted the collapse of the world in

2025 and the Incarnation of the Messiah in 2040); and Nostradamus (who saw the end coming in the form of the sun going supernova).

666	Year of the Devil
1000	Popular belief, fueled by apocalyptic preachers
1033	The year of Christ's Crucifixion, plus 1000 years
1066	Apocalyptic preachers seeing Halley's Comet
1466	Apocalyptic preachers seeing Halley's Comet
1583	R. Harvey, Age of the Spirit of Joachim da Fiore
1666	Popular preachers after the Great London Fire
1707	Assorted French prophets
1843	William Miller
1844	William Miller (second try)
1874	Morton Edgar predicts Millennial Age
1912	Popular belief over Halley's Comet
1950	Henry Adams
1999	Seventh Day Adventists; Jehovah's Witnesses
2000	Malachy; Marian Prophecy of Garabdandal; Marian Prophecy of Fátima; Grand Conjunction (May 4, 2000); Ice Shift (Richard Noone)
2001	Edgar Cayce (Axis Shift)
2012	Mayan Calendar
2013	Incan Calendar
2025	Max Toth predicts the collapse of humanity
2915	Morton Edgar predicts the final test for humanity
3797	Nostradamus
6300	Max Toth predicts the Grand Climacteric

Suggested Reading

The following books are among the many volumes that have been consulted during the writing and compilation of this volume. Readers are encouraged to consult them for additional aspects on the coming years and a variety of interpretations as to what individual prophecies may mean.

Aburdene, Patricia, and John Naisbitt. *Megatrends for Women.* New York: Random House, 1992.

Argüelles, José. *The Mayan Factor.* Santa Fe, N.M.: Bear & Co., 1987.

Baigent, Michael, Richard Leigh, and Henry Lincoln. *The Messianic Legacy.* London: Corgi Books, 1987.

Bell, Daniel. *Towards the Year 2000: Work in Progress.* Boston: Beacon Press, 1969.

Berlitz, Charles. *Doomsday 1999 A.D.* New York: Doubleday, 1981.

Bernbaum, Edwin. *The Way to Shambhala: A Search for the Mythical Kingdom Beyond the Himalayas.* Garden City, N.Y.: Doubleday, Anchor Press, 1980.

Blacker, Carmen, and Michael Loewe, eds. *Ancient Cosmologies.* London: Allen & Unwin, 1975.

Blavatsky, Helena. *Isis Unveiled.* Los Angeles: The Theosophy Co., 1931.

_____. *The Secret Doctrine.* Los Angeles: The Theosophy Co., 1947.

Capra, Fritjof. *The Turning Point.* London: Wildwood House, 1982.

Carter, Mary Ellen. *Edgar Cayce On Prophecy.* New York: Warner Books, 1968.

Cheetham, Erika. *The Prophecies of Nostradamus.* London: Spearman, 1973.

_____. *The Final Prophecies of Nostradamus.* London: Futura, 1990.

Cheiro, Count Louis Hamon. *Cheiro's World Predictions.* Santa Fe, N.M.: Sun Publishing, 1981.

Collin, Rodney. *The Theory of Celestial Influence.* Boulder, Colo.: Shamhala, 1984.

Cohn, Norman. *The Pursuit of the Millennium.* London: Granada, 1970.

Crowley, Aleister. *777 and Other Cabalistic Writings.* New York: Samuel Weiser, 1973.

Davidson, and Aldersmith. *The Great Pyramid: Its Divine Message.* London: Williams & Norgate, 1925.

Denis, Geoffrey. *The End of the World.* London: Eyre & Spottiswoode, 1930.

Edgar, Morton. *The Great Pyramid: Its Time Features.* Glasgow: Bone & Hulley, 1924.

Edmonds, I. G. *Second Sight: People Who Read the Future.* New York: Thomas Nelson, 1977.

Fisher, Joe. *Predictions.* New York: Van Nostrand Reinhold, Co., 1980.

Forman, Henry James. *The Story of Prophecy.* Santa Fe, N.M.: Sun Publishing, 1981.

Fromm, Erich. *To Have or To Be? A New Blueprint for Mankind.* London: Abacus, 1978.

Gattey, Charles. *Prophecy and Prediction in the 20th Century.* Wellingborough: Aquarian Press, 1989.

Glass, Justine. *They Foresaw the Future, The Story of Fulfilled Prophecy.* New York: G.P. Putnam's Son, 1969.

Goodman, Jeffrey. *The Earthquake Generation.* London: Turnstone, 1979.

Green, Owen. *Nuclear Winter.* Cambridge, Mass.: Polity Press, 1985.

Gribbin, John. *Future Weather and the Greenhouse Effect.* London: Delta, Eleanor Friede, 1982.

Gurdjieff, G. I. *All and Everything: Beelzebub's Tales to His Grandson.* New York: Arkana, 1985.

Hall, Manley Palmer. *Secret Teachings of All Ages.* Los Angeles: Philosophical Research Society, 1968.

Hewitt, V.J., and Peter Lorie. *Nostradamus. The End of the Millennium Prophecies: 1992 to 2001.* New York: Simon & Schuster, 1991.

Holzer, Hans. *Prophecies. Visions of the World's Fate: Truths, Possibilities, or Fallacies?* New York: Contemporary Books, 1995.

_____. *The Prophets Speak.* New York: Bobbs-Merrill, 1971.

Hogue, John. *Nostradamus & The Millennium.* London: Bloomsbury, 1987.

_____. *The Millennium Book of Prophecy.* San Francisco: HarperSan Francisco, 1994.

Jochmans, J. R. *Rolling Thunder: The Coming Earth Changes.* Santa Fe, N.M.: Sun Publishing, 1986.

Jung, Carl G. (trans. By H. G. Baynes). *VII Sermones ad Mortuos.* London: Sturat & Watkins, 1963.

Langley, Noel. *Edgar Cayce—The World's Greatest Psychic.* London: The Aquarian Press, HarperCollins, 1989.

Lawrence, D. H. *Apocalypse.* London: Penguin, 1984.

Lemesurier, Peter. *The Armageddon Script: Prophecy in Action.* Shaftesbury, England: Element Books, 1981.

_____. *Gospel of the Stars.* Tisbury, England: Element Books, 1977.

_____. *The Great Pyramid Decoded.* Tisbury, England: Element Books, 1977.

Lewinsohn, Richard. *Prophets and Predictions.* London: Secker and Warbug, 1961.

Lorie, Peter. *The Millennium Planner.* New York: Viking, 1995.

_____. *Nostradamus. The Millennium and Beyond.* New York: Simon & Schuster, 1993.

Mann, A. T. *Millennium Prophecies, Predictions for the Year 2000.* Shaftesbury, England: Element, 1992.

McFadden, Steven. *Profiles in Wisdom: Native Elders Speak About the Earth.* Santa Fe, N.M.: Bear & Co., 1991.

Montgomery, Ruth, with Joanne Garland. *Ruth Montgomery: Herald of the New Age.* N.Y.: Fawcett Crest, 1986.

Montgomery, Ruth. *Aliens Among Us.* New York: Fawcett Crest, 1985.

_____. *Strangers Among Us.* New York: Fawcett Crest, 1979.

_____. *Threshold to Tomorrow.* New York: Fawcett Crest, 1982.

_____. *A World Before.* New York: Fawcett Crest, 1971.

_____. *A World Beyond.* New York: Fawcett Crest, 1971.

Noone, Richard. *5/5/2000 Ice. The Ulitmate Disaster.* New York: Harmony Books, 1971.

Ouspensky, P. D. *In Search of the Miraculous.* London: Harvest, Harcourt Brace Jovanovich Books, 1977.

Paracelsus. *The Prophecies of Paracelsus.* London: Rider, 1974.

Robinson, Lytle. *Edgar Cayce's Story of the Origin and Destiny of Man.* New York.: Berkeley Books, 1976.

Schell, Jonathan. *The Fate of the Earth.* London: Picador, 1982.

Shaw, Eva. *Eve of Destruction, Prophecies, Theories, and Preparations for the End of the World.* Los Angeles: Lowell House, 1995.

Stearn, Jess. *Edgar Cayce: The Sleeping Prophet.* New York: Bantam, 1967.

Steiner, Rudolf. *Cosmic Memory.* San Francisco: Harper & Row, 1959.

_____. *Earthly and Cosmic Man.* London: Rudolf Steiner Publishing, 1948.

Stewart, R. J. *The Prophetic Vision of Merlin.* London: Arkana, 1986.

Toffler, Alvin. *Future Shock.* London: Bodley Head, 1970.

Toth, Max. *Pyramid Prophecies*. Rochester: Destiny Books, 1988.

Trismegistus, Hermes, and Walter Scot, eds. *Hermetica*. Boston: Shambhala, 1985.

Vaughan, Alan. *Patterns in Prophecy*. New York.: Hawthorn Books, 1973.

Wallenchinsky, David. *The Book of Predictions*. New York: William Morrow, 1980.

Ward, Charles A. *Oracles of Nostradamus*. New York: Dorset Press, 1986.

West, John Anthony. *Serpent on the Sky*. New York: Harper & Row, 1979.

Woldben, A. *After Nostradamus* (trans. By Gavin Gibbons). St. Alban's: Granada, 1977.